THE
GARY NUMAN
PRINCIPLE

**Perry
Greenshaw**

THE
GARY NUMAN
PRINCIPLE

**Perry
Greenshaw**

WP
WYMER
PUBLISHING
Bedford, England

First published in Great Britain in 2026
by Wymer Publishing
www.wymerpublishing.co.uk
Tel: 01234 326691
Wymer Publishing is a trading name of Wymer (UK) Ltd

ISBN: 978-1-918419-03-0

Edited by Jerry Bloom

Typeset and Design by Andy Bishop/Tusseheia Creative
Printed and bound by Halstan, Amersham, Buckinghamshire.

Cover photos © Alan Perry Concert Photography

A catalogue record for this book is available from the British Library.

All photos © Alan Perry Concert Photography
Pages 8,10,12,14, 16, 18, 20 & 21, 26, 28, 30, 34, 36-42, 48, 50 & 51
are all from Liverpool Empire Theatre, 25th September 1979.
Pages 60, 62, 64, 78 (top), 79 (bottom) & 81
are all from, Coventry Theatre, 25th September 1980.
Pages 66, 68 & 69, 73-77, 78 (bottom), 79 (top), 80, 82, 84 & 86
are all from Hammersmith Odeon, London, 15th September 1980.
Pages 90-97, & 108
are all from Coventry Theatre, 5th October 1983.

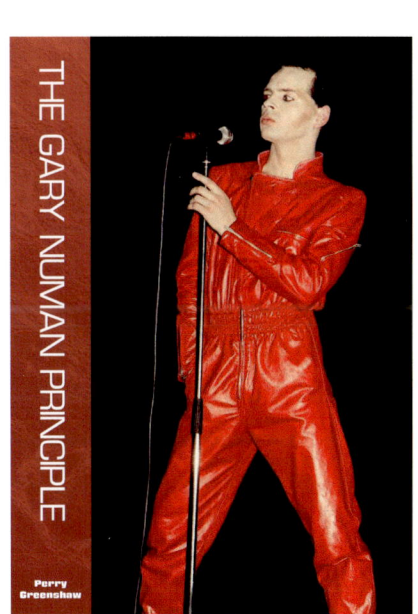

THE GARY NUMAN PRINCIPLE

Perry
Greenshaw

Roll Of Honour

Wymer Publishing duly acknowledges the following people who all put their faith in this publication by pre-ordering it:

Bruce Ashcroft

Sally Carling

Richard Churchward

Sarah Cobb

Simon Cross

Paul Curtis

Jim Dix

Adrian Donaghy

Susan Elliott

Kevin Fishwick

Jon Garland

Kenneth Gray

Julie Groves

John D. Hall

Steve Hallett

Timothy Harrison

Ian Hauton

Derek Hayward

Mark Hornett

David Hughes

Ruth Kane

Steve Kane

Daryl Kent

Jean-Guy Lessire

Gary Lister

Lewis Llewellyn

Tony Lyons

Clive Mcglinchey

Simone Meiser

Rob Milward

Ulrik Naunton

Michael Nibblett

Lorna Potter

Vincent Rojas

Jav Shad

Jane Spilsbury

Peter Steer

Andrew Tranter

Darren Warne

Mark Weatherson

Rosemary Williams

Contents

Introduction

Gary Numan stands as one of the most singular and influential figures in the history of popular music, a visionary artist whose radical reimagining of rock's possibilities helped usher in an entirely new era of electronic sound. Numan has forged a career spanning more than four decades, one characterised by restless innovation, fierce independence, and an unwavering commitment to his distinctive artistic vision. His contribution to music extends far beyond the commercial triumphs of his early career; he fundamentally altered the sonic landscape of popular culture, opening pathways that countless artists would subsequently traverse, and established an aesthetic template that continues to resonate through contemporary music.

The late 1970s represented a pivotal moment in British popular music, a period of extraordinary creativity when the certainties of the preceding decade were being systematically dismantled. Punk had torn through the established order with its raw, confrontational energy, yet within a remarkably short span, its initial impetus had begun to dissipate, leaving behind a vacuum that various emergent movements sought to fill.

It was into this febrile atmosphere that Numan emerged, initially with his band Tubeway Army, bringing with him a sound and sensibility that seemed to arrive from some parallel timeline, simultaneously futuristic and oddly timeless. Where his contemporaries in the post-punk landscape were exploring angular guitar textures and art-school experimentalism, Numan gravitated towards the cold, precise sound of synthesisers, recognising in these instruments a means of expressing something that traditional rock instrumentation could not adequately convey.

Numan's detached, almost affectless vocal delivery and its dystopian lyrical imagery captured the imagination of a British public hungry for something genuinely novel. Much of his early work was so resolutely uncommercial in its construction, so resistant to the conventional wisdom about what constituted a hit single. Numan's artistic universe—a world of urban alienation,

technological anxiety, and emotional disconnection—was rendered in stark electronic tones that seemed to embody the very themes the music explored.

What distinguished Numan from many of his contemporaries was not simply his embrace of electronic technology, but the complete aesthetic vision he constructed around it. His stage persona, with its robotic movements, pale makeup, and thousand-yard stare, seemed to deliberately eschew the traditional markers of rock authenticity— the sweating, guitar-wielding frontman connecting viscerally with the audience. Instead, Numan presented himself as something remote, unknowable, almost inhuman, a figure who seemed to exist, removed from ordinary human experience. This was not mere affectation or gimmickry; it represented a coherent artistic statement about alienation, about the increasing mediation of human experience through technology, about the difficulty of genuine connection in an increasingly mechanised world. His lyrics, often exploring themes of paranoia, isolation, and the breakdown of human relationships, found their perfect vehicle in music that sounded as though it had been created by machines

rather than human hands.

Even as he enjoyed his initial mainstream success, Numan remained something of an outsider figure, someone who seemed fundamentally at odds with the music industry's expectations and conventions. The British music press, in particular, often treated him with barely concealed contempt, dismissing his work as cold, mechanical, emotionally barren— criticisms that rather missed the point of what Numan was attempting to achieve.

Where they saw limitations, Numan saw aesthetic choices; where they heard emptiness, he was crafting precisely calibrated emotional landscapes. This critical hostility would prove to be a recurring feature of his career, yet Numan's response was characteristic: rather than softening his approach to win favour, he doubled down on his vision, becoming if anything more uncompromising as his commercial fortunes waned.

What makes Numan's story particularly compelling is the remarkable renaissance he has experienced in the twenty-first century. Younger artists, many of them not even born when Numan dominated the

12

charts, have cited him as a formative influence, recognising in his early work a pioneering vision that had anticipated so much of contemporary electronic music. Industrial bands, darkwave artists, synthpop revivalists, and even hip-hop producers have acknowledged their debt to Numan's innovations, helping to re-contextualise his contributions and introduce his music to new generations of listeners.

Numan's influence on popular music is both profound and wide-ranging, extending far beyond the narrow confines of electronic pop. His pioneering use of synthesisers as the primary means of musical expression, rather than merely as supplementary colour, helped cement electronic music as a legitimate form in its own right. The aesthetic he developed—the marriage of cold, mechanical sounds with explorations of emotional alienation and technological anxiety—created a template that has been endlessly replicated and refined by subsequent artists. One can hear echoes of Numan's approach in the work of Nine Inch Nails, in the industrial textures of Ministry, in the icy electronics of numerous darkwave and synthwave artists, in the dystopian soundscapes of contemporary electronic producers. Even artists working in ostensibly different genres have acknowledged his impact; the rapper Kanye West sampled "Cars" for his track "Power," introducing Numan's work to hip-hop audiences who might never otherwise have encountered it.

Beyond these direct musical influences, Numan's broader cultural impact deserves recognition. His unflinching exploration of themes relating to technology, alienation, and the erosion of human connection seems remarkably prescient from our current vantage point, in an age dominated by social media, artificial intelligence, and increasing automation. The anxieties he articulated in songs written in the late 1970s and early 1980s—about surveillance, about the dehumanising effects of technology, about the difficulty of maintaining authentic human relationships in an increasingly mediated world—resonate with particular force today. In this sense, Numan was not simply reflecting the concerns of his own moment but anticipating issues that would become central to contemporary discourse.

His career also stands as a testament

14

to the value of artistic integrity and persistence in the face of changing fashions and critical indifference. Numan's refusal to compromise his vision, to moderate his approach in pursuit of commercial acceptance, speaks to a rare kind of artistic courage. Many artists, faced with the kind of commercial decline he experienced in the middle phase of his career, might have either retired from music altogether or attempted to reinvent themselves according to prevailing trends. Numan did neither, continuing instead to plough his own furrow, trusting that his work had value regardless of its immediate reception. That this faith has been vindicated by his late-career renaissance makes his story all the more satisfying, though one suspects that even without this recognition, Numan would have continued making music on his own terms.

Gary Numan's story is one of innovation, persistence, and ultimate vindication. It is the story of an artist who looked towards the future and helped create it, who took sounds that were peripheral and made them central, who constructed a complete artistic vision and remained faithful to it across decades. His contribution to music is not merely historical, a matter of influence exerted upon subsequent generations of artists, though that contribution is substantial enough. Rather, Numan remains a vital, active presence in contemporary music, an artist whose work continues to evolve and whose relevance has, if anything, increased with time. This book seeks to celebrate the full arc of that remarkable journey, from the bedroom experimentation of the teenage Gary to the elder statesman of electronic music he has become.

The Life Machine

Gary Anthony James Webb was born on 8th March 1958 in Hammersmith, West London. His father earned his living as a bus driver for British Airways, operating from the company's base at Heathrow Airport. When Gary reached the age of seven, his family took the significant step of adopting his cousin John, who was actually his father's nephew. This adopted brother would later pursue a career in music himself and eventually perform as a member of Gary's backing band.

Gary's educational journey took him through several institutions in the Surrey and Berkshire areas. He began his schooling at Town Farm Junior School, located in Stanwell, Surrey, before progressing to Ashford County Grammar School and subsequently Slough Grammar School. Following his secondary education, he attended Brooklands Technical College, situated in Weybridge, Surrey, where he continued his studies. During his teenage years, he became involved with the Air Training Corps, and in the period that followed, he moved through a succession of different occupations. These included working as a bus driver at Heathrow Airport, following in his father's footsteps in that regard, operating a forklift truck, fitting air conditioning ventilation systems, and performing clerical duties as an accounts clerk. This varied work experience across different sectors preceded his eventual commitment to a career in music.

Aside from his interest in music Gary was also passionate about planes and from a young age harboured a desire to be a pilot.

At the age of fifteen, Numan received a Gibson Les Paul guitar from his father, an instrument that would become his most prized and cherished possession. During this period, he participated briefly in a variety of different bands and actively sought out opportunities

by examining the advertisements placed in *Melody Maker*, searching for groups he might join. According to his own account, Gary auditioned for the position of guitarist with a band called The Jam, who at that time had not yet achieved fame or recognition, though this audition proved unsuccessful. He subsequently became a member of two bands, Mean Street and the Lasers, and it was during his time with the latter that he encountered Paul Gardiner, who would become an important musical collaborator.

The Lasers would undergo a transformation and emerge as Tubeway Army, with the line-up featuring his uncle Jess Lidyard taking the role of drummer whilst Gardiner remained with the group as bass player. This incarnation of the band succeeded in securing a recording contract with Beggars Banquet Records, an independent label created in 1977 by Martin Mills and Nick Austin. It would prove significant in launching Numan's career.

Mills and Austin's decision to create Beggars Banquet was influenced and encouraged by the do-it-yourself ethos that characterised the British punk rock movement, which at that particular moment was experiencing the peak of its cultural influence and widespread popularity.

The inaugural band they signed was The Lurkers, an English punk group, and the very first release that Beggars Banquet issued was a seven-inch single featuring the tracks "Shadow" and "Love Story." The label also released what was billed as the first solo album under the name *Duffo* by Jeff Duff, an Australian vocalist who had previously performed with big-band ensembles.

The hits generated by Tubeway Army and Gary Numan provided crucial financial stability and ensured the continued viability and future prospects of Beggars Banquet, establishing it as a significant independent force in the British music industry.

During his early career, and prior to becoming known as Gary Numan he had previously adopted the pseudonym Valerian. This stage name was likely chosen as a reference to the protagonist of Valérian and Laureline, a French science fiction comic book series. However, he selected the name Numan after noticing an advertisement in the Yellow Pages telephone directory. The advertisement was for a plumbing contractor whose surname was Neumann, and Numan adapted this name for his own use, creating the stage identity by which he would soon become famous.

THAT'S TOO BAD
BY TUBEWAY ARMY
ON BEGGARS BANQUET
RECORDS

Looked up and the camera eye is searching my room
The TV screen is calling me but for what or whom?
Please Mister, do be careful — I'm so fragile
Maybe they'll let me down to Speedy's place for a while

Chorus
Oh, oh well, that's too bad
Oh, oh well, that's too bad
Oh, oh well, that's too bad
Oh, oh well, that's too bad

Talk a lot, a sign of fear, I thought you should know
I can see pictures of me — well, they're so-so
I'll come on to the leader like I'm some hero
He'll laugh and raise his dying eyes and then tell me to go

Repeat chorus

1920 flashbacks for an hour or more
Of crazy actors hiding in the doorways top floor
Machines scream in anger from a thousand dead ends
I turn my face, I crawl away, I look for a friend

Repeat chorus to fade

Words and music by Valerian
Reproduced by permission Beggars Banquet/Andrew Heath
Music Ltd.

Requested by Leigh Griffiths, Swansea.

GARY NUMAN

LIVING ORNAMENTS '79
BEGA 24
LIVING ORNAMENTS '80
BEGA 25
LIVING ORNAMENTS BOX SET
BOX SET 1

ALL AVAILABLE ON CASSETTE
LIMITED EDITIONS

Beggars Banquet

10

ME, I DISCONNECT FROM YOU

Gary Numan now only talks to people he trusts. Frank Drake and Peter Gilbert give us an exclusive report on the latest in his controversial career.

WE PUSH the appropriate button on the wall outside Gary Numan's West London flat. After we announce our names through the grill of the outside security microphone, a buzz automatically opens the front door. Once inside, a lift whisks us quietly to the third floor. A knock on the door, an eye at the security peephole and we are inside Gary Numan's apartment.

Gary, dressed in a T shirt and jeans, is relaxed and chatty as he sits cross-legged on the floor. It's been exactly a year since we first chatted with Gary in a wine bar in the London suburb of Ealing. In that time he's become famous and the hero of hundreds of fans — is it frustrating for him now that he's reached his goal?

"Oh, you mean the 'now I need new reasons' bit? I wouldn't say it's frustrating, although I have noticed that I get very restless a lot of the time. I'm back to looking for something again, like I was before. Now I sit here for hours and hours, day after day, looking for something more.

"I still want to do something in films, but I'm not sure whether I'm confident enough, whether I've got enough talent to take it further than just one experiment, or that I could write enough short stories to take it any further than one collection of twelve.

"I don't even feel confident that I can go on writing songs sometimes. In fact, I feel very unconfident about the whole thing!"

Gary smiles at his last remark and we realise that he is a lot more relaxed these days. We asked him how he would describe himself?

"I feel like a very old man in a very young body."

Why old?

"I just feel old, I feel old and wise."

Is this because your success happened too quickly for you?

"I think I have experienced more at my age than maybe is wise for me. Maybe someone else of my age could take it all in, quite easily. As it is, for me personally, I find it a lot to take in. I wouldn't say I'm driven to insanity by it or anything like that, I just find it a lot to take in."

Gary pauses for a moment in order to explain himself better, and he thinks deeply before continuing.

"Maybe it's the same for eveyone at any age and I'm just going through that, but I think I would need to be few more years older before I could put up with all the knocking."

But doesn't the very fact that you have got where you are prove to those people that knock you, that they are not really important?

"Yes, it does, but I have never said that they are important to that extent. Not at this level they're not important, but it still doesn't alter the fact that everytime I pick up a paper I read some snide comment or other

and that upsets me, and I get depressed about it naturally.

"I don't read papers anymore because each week they're tearing me down and that gets on my nerves after a while."

THE INSECURE, paranoid, weak-willed impression given by the media to describe Gary Numan in the late '70s certainly doesn't apply to the person now sitting before us in front of the television with the sound turned down.

We asked him if he still feels isolated from people generally? Gary still hasn't lost that sometimes naive honesty which is apparent in his answer to our question.

"Yeah, more than ever!"

But what about those at that write to you and go to your gigs, there's a lot of warmth there surely?

"Yes, maybe, but it's all very short lived isn't it? I'm not stupid enough to think that they are going to write letters to me saying they're going to love me for ever, say next year, because I know damn well that they probably won't.

"So all that you've mentioned isn't really any consolation at all because it's all sheer fantasy on their part and this makes me feel possibly lonelier than I would've felt if I had never got it in the first place."

We pointed out that, nevertheless, many people feel warm towards him for a number of reasons. Does Gary see and feel that warmth at all?

"I can see it and I can feel it but what I'm saying is, it's only real for today. It's not like loving somebody and loving that somebody for the next 50 years; it isn't that real.

"Most of it comes from young girls or sometimes young boys and it's sheer childhood fantasies and teenage crushes on the latest pop star. Y'know, they stick up a pretty picture and they fancy it and that's about as deep as the love they have for me goes and for very, very few of them it's anything more than that."

Has success changed you at all?

"Yes, it's made me much lonelier than I was before." That's very sad to hear you say that?

"Maybe it is, but it won't last forever. It won't always be that way. It's the price I'm paying now which I can take advantage of in the future; it's not such a big price to pay, really.

"Obviously we're talking about it on the dark side at the moment but there's lots of good things about it too. I suppose I tend to think more about the bad points," (Gary laughs) "that way I can write more songs."

IN HIS official fan club newsletter, it stated that he would be appearing on the Kenny Everett Video Show on New Years Eve, singing a version of "I Die, You Die." We wanted to know why he didn't appear on the show. What went wrong?

"Well, the reason we said we was going to do it was because we were asked by Thames Television to do it, and they said it would be for the New Years Eve show.

"We then went and filmed it and spent a whole day on it. I was dancing for about eight hours without a break filming this bloody thing, and there were promises all round that I could go and help with the editing.

"It was definitely going to be on the New Years Eve show because it was 'Looking into the 80's', and there was going to be people from the 70's like Bowie. And as it was New Years Eve, it was going to show what was happening in the 80's, that sort of thing. This was going to be us, that was our part in it.

"I went down to watch Bowie do his bit after we'd done ours

and I got thrown out. I was told by the director that Bowie didn't want me there, which was fair enough, I suppose."

Just you personally or everyone else as well?

"Well, me to start with and then apparently he was upset by it and then everyone had to go. Later on he stormed off and wouldn't do a sketch with Kenny Everett. The next thing we heard was, we were not being used at all.

"Then we were told that what we did and what Bowie did was not working well together. That was rubbish because I saw what Bowie did, because I was there, and they are nothing like each other at all. There is no way that they could not have gone together.

"They said they they wanted us to do the show in the first place because it would have been good to have a confrontation between David Bowie and me on the very last programme of the year, just to compare if nothing else.

"And I was all for that, because it would've cleared the air once and for all, and hopefully people would have realised, seeing us side by side, that we are really nothing alike at all. The way Bowie moves and sings and his music, is nothing like the way I move and sing and my music!

"Now the fact that he wore a black leather jumpsuit — and I wouldn't dare say he was copying me by wearing black — I wouldn't dare say that!

"Anyway, to go on from that, we found out later that the man who directs the Everett show also works with Bowie during the year on his own videos, so obviously there is a big cash involvement.

"And then we all came to the conclusion, which wasn't denied at the time by the producer of the show, that Bowie didn't want us on it and he had pulled this cash lever with the director to get us off it. And that seems to be what happened.

"The last thing we heard from Thames was that they had changed the format of the show and instead of looking into the 80's, it was now decided to look back at the 70's. But that was still not a good enough reason to take us off it because we were the last pop stars of the 70's, so we should've been on it for that reason, more than any other.

"So whatever reason they said, the fact is we were not on it and there was no reason for us not to have been on it, except that Bowie didn't want us on it and he used his influence with the director to get us off it. Now that may or may not be true."

IF WHAT Gary is saying is true, then surely he must be very disillusioned with Bowie?

"Completely! I look at him in a completely different light now, to how I saw him before. I've lost a lot of respect for him because,

if that's how he got where he is today, by doing that sort of thing to other people, then he's a shitbag!"

But doesn't Gary expect too much honesty from other people?

"No, I don't expect them to be taken off shows just because he's worried about opposition, especially as I'm considered by the press and most Bowie fans alike to be just a cheap Bowie rip-off anyway. If I am a cheap Bowie rip-off, why is he scared of having me on the same programme?

"Obviously I'm not a cheap Bowie rip-off and I must be the biggest competition he has had in about the last seven or eight years, and what's more, he's worried about it!"

If this is the case, that Bowie regards you as a threat, how does it make you feel?

"I'm pleased! I'm just disappointed that he should have to resort to such measures because I would like to have

spoken to him and met the man. I've idolised that bloke for seven years and the first chance I get to meet him, he decides to do that."

GARY NUMAN: still as outspoken, still as honest, still as interesting. Now he's speaking out more, against the press, the corruption in the bizz. A character that is easily underestimated by those who think they are so important!

As for Gary, he's doing okay and he's doing it the right way and doesn't that just get up his critics' noses? Don't it just!

Among the very first of Gary Numan's fans, Peter Gilbert and Francis Drake run a fanzine called "In The City". Issue 14 is now available containing more on Gary Numan, Adam & The Ants, Ultravox, Poison Girls and more, and costs 40p (including post) from: In The City, c/o Compendium Books, 234 Camden High Street, LONDON NW1.

My Shadow In Vain

With Tubeway Army Numan established himself as a prominent figure during the late 1970s through his multiple roles as the lead vocalist, guitarist, songwriter and producer. Following their decision to adopt a musical style aligned with punk rock, Tubeway Army's first release for Beggars Banquet was their single, "That's Too Bad," released in February 1978. It represented the band's attempt to create punk music with commercial appeal and accessibility.

This initial release was followed by recording sessions in March 1978 during which the band laid down enough material for a complete album's worth of material, but these recordings were only for demonstration purposes. However, they would eventually see official release in 1984 under the title *The Plan*. Meanwhile, a second single, "Bombers," was subsequently issued, but like its predecessor, it failed to make any impact on the charts or achieve a chart position.

Both of these early singles were given a second commercial life when they were reissued together in 1979 as a gatefold double-pack release, packaged as a single unit. Then in 1983, "That's Too Bad" received yet another re-release, and on this occasion the single managed to achieve a modest degree of chart success, reaching number 97 on the UK singles chart. This belated chart appearance came some five years after the track's original release and demonstrated the increased interest in Numan's early work following his subsequent mainstream success.

In 1978 Numan started learning to fly at Blackbushe Aerodrome in Surrey but the success of Tubeway Army delayed his chances of securing his pilot's licence.

26

The self-titled debut studio album by Tubeway Army, which was oriented towards the new wave style, appeared in November 1978. The album completely sold out its limited pressing run and served to introduce Numan's deep interest in dystopian science fiction themes and synthesiser technology. A pivotal moment occurred during the recording sessions for this album when Numan discovered a Moog synthesiser that had been left behind in the studio by another artist or session. This chance encounter marked the beginning of the band's gradual transition towards an electronic-based sound that would come to define their work.

Tubeway Army's third single, "Down In The Park" was released in 1979 and featured a dark thematic content delivered at a deliberately slow tempo. Despite failing to register any position on the charts upon its release, the track would go on to become one of Numan's most enduring compositions and has been covered by numerous artists over the subsequent decades.

The song gained additional exposure when it was included alongside other contemporary hit recordings on the soundtrack for *Times Square*, an American drama film released in 1980. Furthermore, a live performance version was featured in *Urgh! A Music War*, a

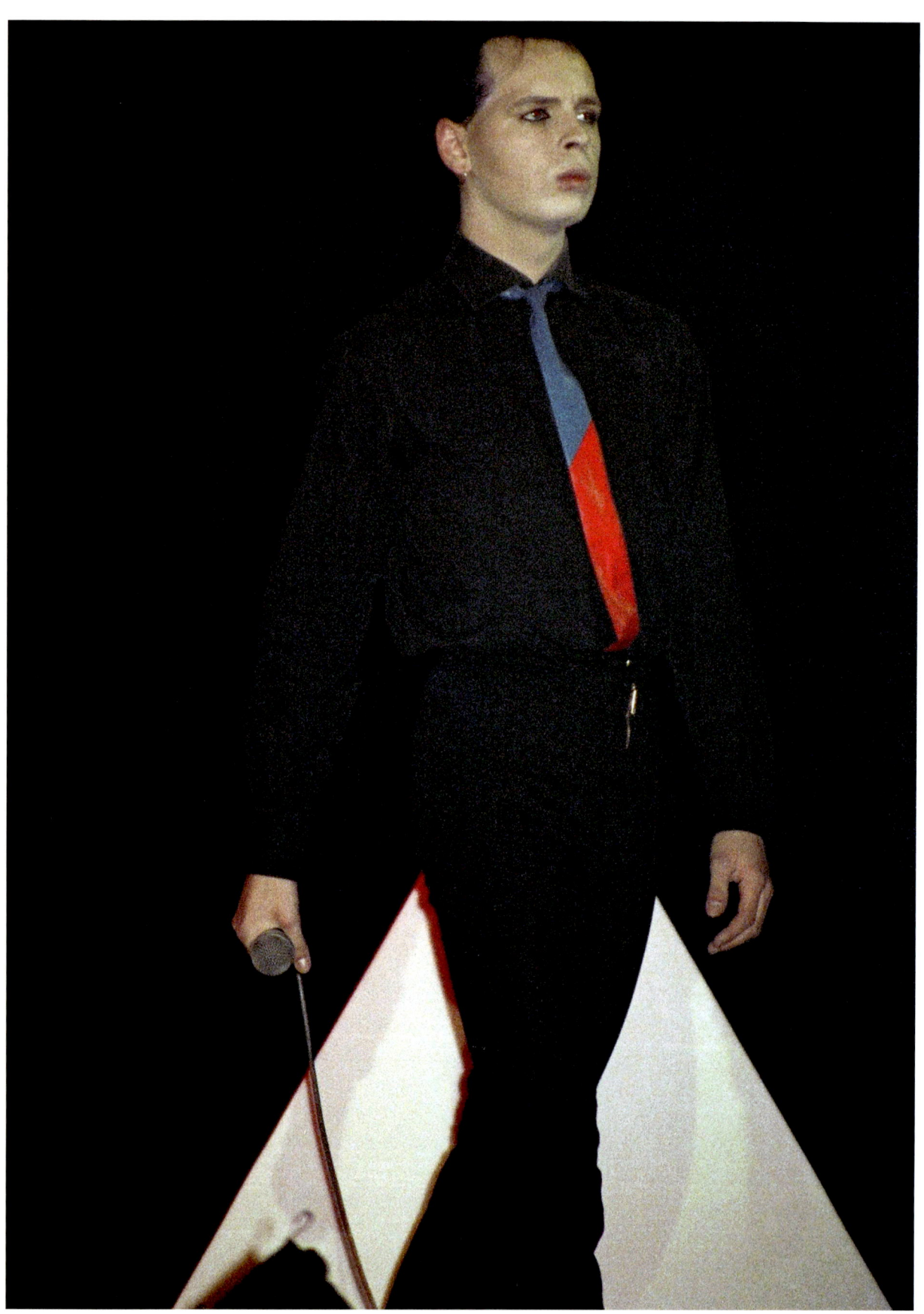

28

British concert film that was released in 1982. The film, produced by Michael White and Lyndall Hobbs featured a host of artists, including Orchestral Manoeuvres In The Dark, XTC, UB40, Echo & the Bunnymen, The Police and many more.

"Down In The Park" stands as one of Gary Numan's most uncompromising and disturbing compositions, a track that pushed the boundaries of what popular music might address both thematically and sonically. Its failure to connect commercially at the time of release is perhaps unsurprising given its deliberately confrontational nature, and its refusal to offer any concessions to radio-friendliness or mainstream palatability. This was music designed not to please but to unsettle, to create a sense of profound unease, to force the listener to confront disturbing possibilities about where human society might be heading.

The sonic construction of "Down In The Park" was built around atmosphere and mood, creating a soundworld that was claustrophobic, threatening and oppressive. The tempo was deliberately slow, almost funereal, giving the track a sense of inexorable movement towards some dreadful conclusion. This wasn't music that hurried; it took its time, allowing each element to register fully, creating space for the listener to absorb the full horror of what was being described. The sound was cold, metallic, processed. There was no warmth here, no human touch; the music announced itself as coming from machines, as embodying the technological alienation it would explore thematically.

Numan's vocal delivery on "Down In The Park" was perhaps his most affectless, most deliberately detached. He sang as though reporting from a great distance, describing horrors with the flat, emotionless tone of someone who had become so inured to violence and degradation that they could no longer muster appropriate emotional responses. This disconnect between the disturbing content being described and the apparent calmness of the delivery created a profoundly unsettling effect, suggesting a narrator who had been so damaged by their environment that normal human responses had been systematically eroded. The voice seemed almost to float above the dense synthesiser backing, isolated and alone, connected to nothing, expressing an alienation so complete that even horror could no longer penetrate it.

Lyrically, the song served to crystallise and bring into sharp focus the

dystopian science fiction concept that formed the thematic foundation of the entire *Replicas* album–Tubeway Army's second release. The track's narrative and imagery drew heavily upon the influence of writers such as J. G. Ballard and Philip K. Dick, whose works had clearly made a significant impression on Numan's creative vision.

The song tells the story of a park situated in a futuristic setting where violent spectacles unfold for public entertainment. In this imagined world, Machmen–androids that have been constructed with human skin to make them appear organic–and various machines systematically kill human beings whilst spectators observe the carnage and violence from the safety and comfort of a nearby restaurant establishment called "Zom Zoms."

These spectators are accompanied by their numerically designated robotic companions or "friends," as referenced in the lyrics, with a friend called Five, which explicitly names one such numbered artificial being. The name of the restaurant, "Zom Zoms" was not chosen arbitrarily but was directly inspired by recurring references to the Zum Zum restaurant chain that appeared in "Scumbag," a song by the glam rock artist Jobriath.

"Down In The Park" exemplified and was entirely characteristic of the thematic preoccupations that dominated Numan's work during this particular period of his career. His approach to technology was notably ambivalent and complex, simultaneously embracing the possibilities it offered whilst also expressing deep-seated fear and anxiety about its implications and consequences. This duality–the attraction to and repulsion from technological advancement–ran through much of his early work and gave it a psychological complexity often absent from more straightforwardly utopian or dystopian treatments of similar themes.

In terms of vocal approach and delivery, the track represented a significant departure from much of the contemporary post-punk music that surrounded it, as well as marking a shift from Numan's own earlier releases. His vocals on "Down In The Park" were deliberately understated and underplayed, consciously avoiding the more prominent, aggressive, or emotionally demonstrative vocal styles that characterised much punk and post-punk music. This restrained vocal approach meant that the burden of evoking the song's emotional content

USA

Japan

Spain

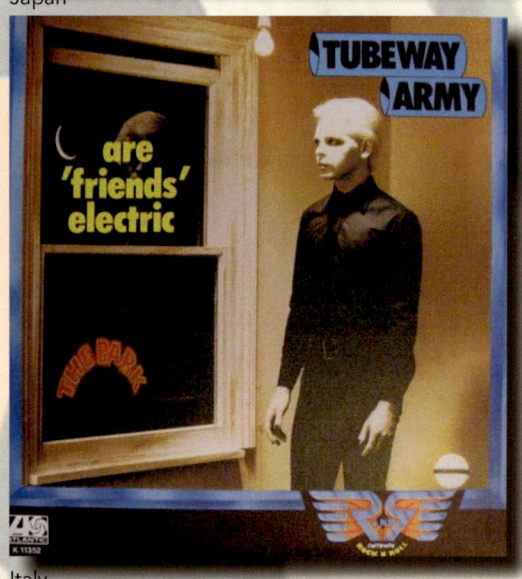

Italy

UK Tape

and atmosphere fell primarily upon the instrumental arrangement. The slow-paced and stately synthesiser work became the primary vehicle for creating and sustaining the track's profoundly melancholic atmosphere, with the electronic instrumentation doing much of the emotional work that in conventional rock music would typically be carried by the vocal performance.

In the context of 1979, "Down In The Park" represented an extreme outlier, a piece of popular music that pushed darkness and disturbing content further than virtually anything else in the charts or on the radio. Punk had certainly explored transgressive themes and imagery, but even punk's most provocative moments typically maintained a certain cartoonish quality, a sense that the shock was part of the performance, not to be taken entirely seriously. "Down In The Park" offered no such reassurance. Its horrors were presented matter-of-factly, without editorialising, without moral commentary, leaving the listener to draw their own conclusions about the world being described and its relationship to our own.

Following Tubeway Army's appearance in a television advertisement for Lee Cooper jeans, which featured them performing a jingle with the lyrics "Don't Be A Dummy," the band released the single "Are 'Friends' Electric?" in May 1979. The single's chart performance began modestly, entering the UK charts at the relatively low position of number 71. However, it demonstrated remarkable staying power and steadily climbed the rankings, ultimately reaching the number one position by the end of June. The single remained at the summit of the charts for four consecutive weeks, an impressive achievement for such an unconventional track.

The Britain of early 1979 was a nation emerging from what had become known as the "Winter of Discontent," a period of widespread industrial action and public sector strikes that had brought the country to a virtual standstill during the closing months of 1978 and the opening weeks of 1979. Images of uncollected rubbish piling up in the streets, of the dead going unburied, of hospitals turning away all but emergency cases, had created a sense of national crisis and contributed substantially to the Labour government's defeat in the general election of May 1979.

Margaret Thatcher's Conservative Party took power promising to reverse British decline, to curb trade union power, and to create an enterprise culture that would replace what they characterised as the sclerotic consensus politics of the post-war period. The optimism that accompanied this change of government was, however, tempered

by anxiety about what such fundamental restructuring might entail, by uncertainty about whether British society could be remade without tearing apart the social fabric that had held the nation together through the difficult post-war decades.

It was into this febrile atmosphere of endings and uncertain beginnings that "Are 'Friends' Electric?" was released, and whilst Numan's work was never overtly political in the manner of, say, The Clash or Billy Bragg, the track's themes of alienation, paranoia, and the breakdown of human connection resonated powerfully with a society that seemed to be fragmenting before people's eyes. The song articulated anxieties that many felt but few had found ways to express, giving voice to a peculiarly contemporary form of urban dread, a sense that the city had become a hostile environment where genuine human connection was increasingly difficult, where trust had broken down, where everyone was potentially a threat.

Speaking to *The Guardian* in 2014, Numan said of the song's lyrics: "All my early songs were about being alone or misunderstood. As a teenager, I'd been sent to a child psychiatrist and put on medication. I had Asperger's and saw the world differently. I immersed myself in sci-fi writers: Philip K Dick, JG Ballard. The lyrics came from short stories I'd written about what London would be like in thirty years. These machines— "friends"—come to the door. They supply services of various kinds, but your neighbours never know what they really are since they look human. The one in the song is a prostitute, hence the inverted commas. It was released in May 1979 and sold a million copies. I had a No. 1 single with a song about a robot prostitute and no one knew."

This ambiguity was central to the track's power and its broader cultural significance. "Are 'Friends' Electric?" could be read on multiple levels simultaneously. On the surface, it told a story about urban alienation and the difficulty of genuine connection, about encountering someone who seemed to offer companionship but who turned out to be something other than they appeared.

The track's exploration of the boundary between human and artificial, between authentic emotion and its simulation, proved remarkably prescient. In 1979, these concerns might have seemed primarily science fictional, extrapolations of existing trends into an imagined future. Four decades later, in an age of social media, artificial intelligence, and increasingly sophisticated simulation technologies, the questions "Are 'Friends' Electric?" raised have become unavoidably concrete. We conduct our relationships increasingly through technological mediation, interacting with others through screens and interfaces. We struggle to distinguish genuine human connection from its simulation. We wonder whether the personas we encounter online represent authentic selves or carefully constructed performances. The anxieties Numan articulated in "Are 'Friends' Electric?" have not diminished but intensified, making the track seem less like a period piece and more like an uncannily accurate prediction of concerns that would become central to contemporary life.

36

37

38

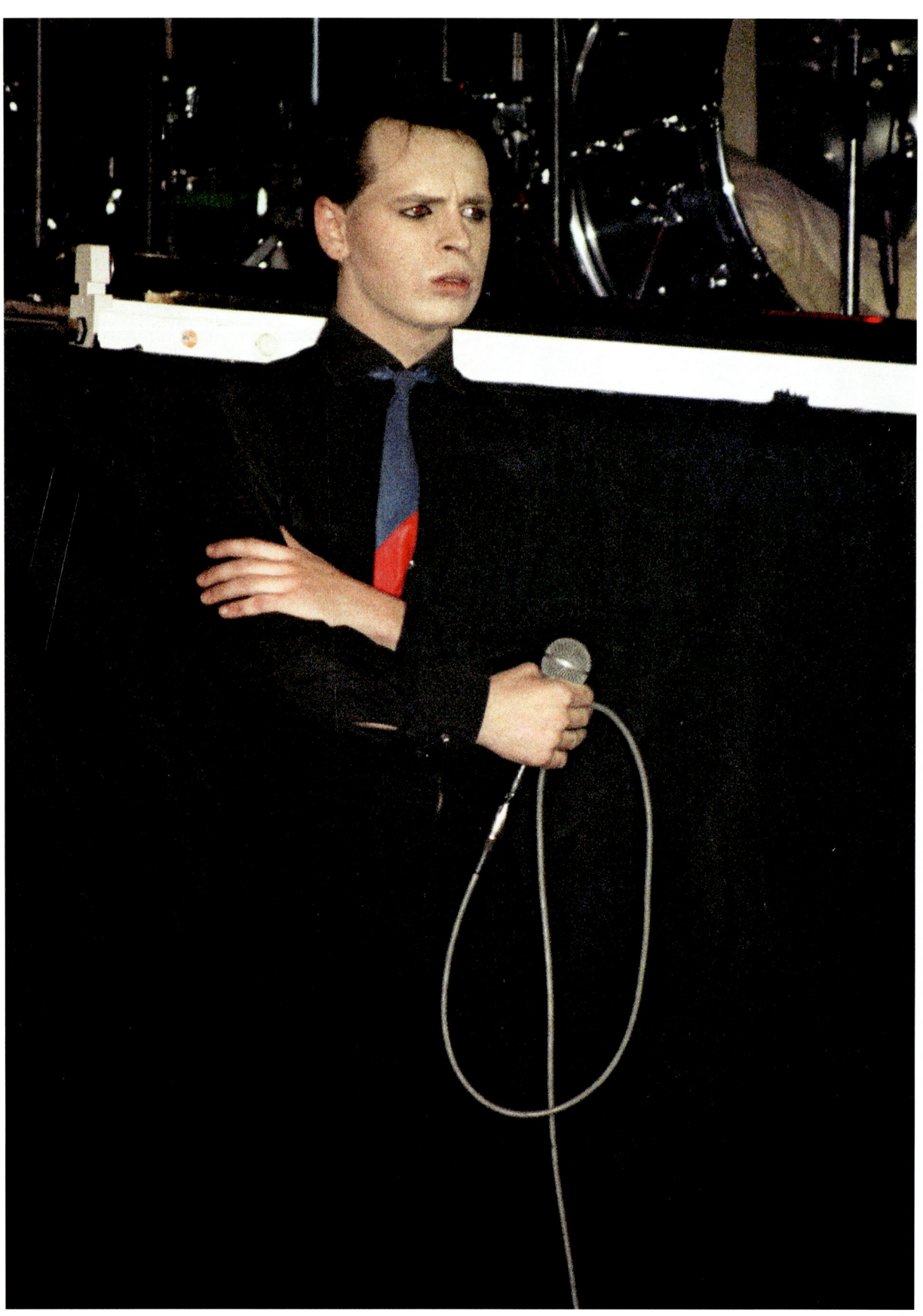

41

Observer

In July of the same year, the parent studio album from which "Are 'Friends' Electric?" was taken, entitled *Replicas*, also achieved the number one position on the albums chart, cementing Numan's breakthrough into mainstream commercial success and establishing him as a major force in British popular music.

At this juncture in his career, Numan was in the process of recording his forthcoming studio album and had assembled a new backing band to support this work. This new line-up included Chris Payne, whom he had recruited to play keyboards, and Cedric Sharpley, who took on the role of drummer.

Despite being at the very pinnacle of his commercial success at this time, Numan made the unconventional decision to premiere four new songs during a session for John Peel's radio programme in June 1979. This choice meant that rather than focusing his promotional efforts on the current album that was enjoying chart success, he was instead showcasing entirely new material. It was also at this point that the Tubeway Army group name was abandoned, with Numan choosing to move forward under his own name as a solo artist rather than continuing to operate under the band identity that had brought him his initial breakthrough.

In September of that year, "Cars" climbed to the number one position in the UK charts. The single also found considerable commercial success when it was released in North American markets, particularly in Canada, spending two weeks at the number one position on the Canadian RPM charts. In the United States, the track reached number nine in 1980, representing a significant American breakthrough.

Both "Cars" and the 1979 studio album *The Pleasure Principle* marked a departure from the Tubeway Army branding, as both were released under Numan's own stage name rather than the group identity he had previously used. The album achieved the number one position in the UK album charts, and its commercial success was followed by a tour called The Touring Principle, which sold out its entire run of dates. This tour generated a concert video that has

frequently been cited and recognised as the first full-length commercial music video release, representing a significant moment in the development of music video as a commercial format.

The Pleasure Principle was notable for its unusual sonic construction—it was fundamentally a rock album in structure and approach, yet it contained no guitar parts whatsoever. Instead of employing guitars, Numan utilised synthesisers that were connected to various effects units, allowing him to achieve a distinctive sound that was distorted, phased, and had a metallic tonal quality. This innovative approach to rock instrumentation demonstrated that traditional rock structures could be maintained whilst completely abandoning conventional rock instrumentation.

A second single, "Complex," was taken from the album and this too achieved chart success, reaching number six on the UK singles chart, further consolidating Numan's position as one of the most commercially successful artists of the period.

The sonic landscape of 1979 was remarkably diverse, characterised by a degree of stylistic fragmentation that reflected the broader cultural

uncertainties of the period. Punk, which had seemed so revolutionary just two years earlier, had largely exhausted its initial impetus, with many of its key figures either disbanded, dead, or pursuing new directions.

The Sex Pistols had imploded in spectacular fashion; The Clash were evolving towards a more expansive sound that incorporated reggae and other influences; post-punk bands like Joy Division, Gang of Four, and Wire were exploring darker, more experimental territories.

Simultaneously, disco remained a commercial force despite mounting backlash, particularly in America where the infamous "Disco Demolition Night" in July 1979 had crystallised anti-disco sentiment into something approaching a cultural movement. Meanwhile, ska and two-tone were enjoying a revival through bands like The Specials and Madness, offering a different kind of British pop sensibility, one rooted in multiculturalism and a knowing engagement with musical history.

It was into this fractured landscape that "Cars" came, and it sounded like nothing else on the radio. The track opened with a synthesiser line that was both immediately memorable and strangely unsettling, a repeated motif that established the song's mechanical, insistent character. There were no guitars, no conventional rock instrumentation whatsoever; instead, Numan had constructed the entire piece from layers of synthesisers. The rhythm was provided not by a drummer but by a drum machine, lending the track a metronomic precision that felt simultaneously hypnotic and vaguely threatening. Over this foundation, Numan's vocal delivery was coolly detached, as though he were reporting from behind glass, observing rather than participating in the emotional content of the lyrics.

The production aesthetic of "Cars" represented a deliberate rejection of the values that had dominated rock music for the preceding decade. Where rock orthodoxy prised warmth, authenticity, and the supposedly unmediated expression of human emotion through traditional instrumentation, "Cars" embraced coldness, artificiality, and technological mediation. The synthesiser sounds were not attempting to imitate acoustic instruments; they announced themselves as electronic, as manufactured, as fundamentally artificial. This was not music that sought

47

48

to replicate the experience of musicians playing together in a room; it was music that could only exist through the intervention of electronic technology, music that seemed to be made by machines as much as by a human creator. In an era when the synthesiser was still viewed with suspicion by rock purists, when electronic instrumentation was often dismissed as somehow less legitimate than guitars and drums, this represented a bold aesthetic statement.

The lyrical content of "Cars" complemented its sonic qualities perfectly, exploring themes of isolation, paranoia, and the desire for safety in a threatening world. The central image—of finding security inside a locked car, viewing the dangerous outside world from behind glass and metal—resonated on multiple levels. On the surface, it could be read as a straightforward narrative about urban anxiety, about the fear of crime and violence that had become increasingly prominent in British discourse during the troubled 1970s. The decade had been marked by economic crisis, industrial unrest, power cuts, the three-day week, and a general sense that British society was in decline, that the post-war settlement was unravelling. The imagery of retreating into a private, sealed space away from external threats spoke directly to these anxieties.

According to Numan, the song's lyrics were inspired by an incident of road rage: "I was in traffic in London once and had a problem with some people in front. They tried to beat me up and get me out of the car. I locked the doors and eventually drove up on the pavement and got away from them. It's kind of to do with that. It explains how you can feel safe inside a car in the modern world... When you're in it, your whole mentality is different... It's like your own little personal empire with four wheels on it."

Yet the song's meaning extended beyond this literal reading. The car as sanctuary could also be understood as a metaphor for emotional withdrawal, for the difficulty of human connection, for the desire to observe life from a safe distance rather than risking genuine engagement. The repeated line "Here in my car, I feel safest of all" suggested not triumph or comfort but a kind of melancholy resignation, an acknowledgement that genuine safety could only be achieved through isolation. The car became a bubble, a privatised space that protected its occupant from the chaos and unpredictability of human interaction. In this reading, "Cars" was not simply about physical danger but about emotional vulnerability, about the appeal of shutting oneself away from the messiness and pain that intimate human contact inevitably brings.

Down in the park
Where the machmen
Meet the machines
And play kill by numbers
Down in the park
With a friend called five

I was in a car crash
Or was it the war
But I've never been
Quite the same
Little white lies
Like I was there

Come to zom zoms
A place to eat
Like it was built
In one day
You can watch the humans
Trying to run

Oh look
There's a rape machine
I'd go outside
If he'd look the other way
You wouldn't believe
The things they do

Down in the park
Where the chant is
Death, death, death
Until the sun cries morning
Down in the park
With friends of mine

We are not lovers
We are not
Romantics
We are here to serve you
A different face
But the words never change

Request Spot

ARTIST TUBEWAY ARMY

SONG DOWN IN THE PARK

LABEL BEGGARS BANQUET

YEAR 1979

REQUESTED BY SARAH DONADEL

KNOWLE, BRISTOL

BEST MALE ARTIST

1. GARY NUMAN

BEST SINGLE

1. ARE FRIENDS ELECTRIC, GARY NUMAN, BEGGARS BANQUET

NEW HOPE FOR 1980

1. GARY NUMAN

BORE OF THE YEAR

2. GARY NUMAN

SEX SYMBOL

4. Gary Numan

BEST BAND

10. Tubeway Army

BEST ALBUM

2. REPLICAS, GARY NUMAN, BEGGARS BANQUET

BEST RECORD SLEEVE

2. REPLICAS, TUBEWAY ARMY, BEGGARS BANQUET

PRETENTIOUS PRAT

1. GARY NUMAN

BEST GIG

5. Gary Numan

DEAD ROCK STAR OF ALL TIME

9. Gary Numan

THANKS A LOT.

Gary Numan x

THIS WRECKAGE

By Gary Numan on Beggars Banquet Records

And what if God's dead?
We must have done something wrong
This dark facade ends
We're independent from someone

This wreckage I call me
Would like to frame your voice
This wreckage I call me
Would like to meet you, meet you
Soon

We write suggestions
Suggesting fading to silence
And that must please you
My mirrors tarnished with "no-help"

This wreckage I call me
Would like to frame your voice
This wreckage I call me
Would like to meet you, meet you
Soon

別れよう
(Mou wakareyo)
(Mou wakareyo)

Turn out, these eyes
Wipe off, my face
Erase me

Replay the end
It's all just show
Erase you

I need to, I need to, I need to

This wreckage I call me
Would like to frame your voice
This wreckage I call me
Would like to leave you, leave you
Leave you, leave you
Soon

別れよう
(Mou wakareyo)

Repeat to fade

Words and music by Gary Numan
Reproduced by permission Numan Music Ltd.

SMASH
HITS
FORTNIGHTLY
November 15-28 1979
30p

CHIC
UNDERTONES

Words to the
TOP SINGLES
including

A Message To You Rudy
Diamond Smiles
Ladies Night

The Selecter
Public Image Ltd.
in colour

JAM
LPs
to be won

GARY
NUMAN

56

This theme of alienation and disconnection was, of course, central to much of the most interesting music emerging in the late 1970s. Joy Division were exploring similar territories, though through very different sonic means, mining a vein of existential despair that would reach its apotheosis in their 1980 album *Closer*. The post-punk movement more broadly was characterised by a rejection of rock's traditional celebration of community and collective experience, favouring instead explorations of isolation, anomie, and psychological distress. What distinguished Numan's approach was the way in which his musical means perfectly embodied his thematic concerns. Where Joy Division's music retained elements of rock's traditional instrumentation–Ian Curtis's anguished vocals were supported by Peter Hook's melodic bass, Bernard Sumner's atmospheric guitar, and Stephen Morris's propulsive drumming–Numan dispensed with these human elements almost entirely, creating music that sounded as isolated and mechanical as the experiences it described.

The commercial success of "Cars" was remarkable given how uncompromising it was in both sound and content.

Despite this commercial success "Cars" was not music designed to please; it was music designed to unsettle, to create a particular atmosphere and mood. Yet it connected with audiences in a way that more conventional pop offerings did not. Part of this success undoubtedly lay in the sheer memorability of the track's central synthesiser hook, a melody that lodged itself in the listener's consciousness and refused to leave. The song had an almost hypnotic quality, its repetitive structure creating a trance-like effect that was both compelling and slightly uncomfortable.

One could not easily ignore "Cars"; it demanded attention through the very starkness of its construction.

Although the music appealed to a more serious audience, hit records also ensured Numan had a significant following of the more run-of-the-mill pop-orientated fan base. This saw regular coverage in magazines such as the young girls' publication *Jackie*. The issue published on 1st September '79 was less concerned with the music but reported that Numan "once wore an old green parachute suit that had holes in it, a red beret, blue Doc Martin boots and a black patent belt. It was horrible!"

The Joy Circuit

In 1980, Numan secured his third UK number one with the release of *Telekon*. Prior to the album's appearance, two singles were issued—"We Are Glass" and "I Die: You Die"—both of which achieved strong chart performances, reaching number five and number six respectively on the UK charts. Following the album's release, a single titled "This Wreckage," which was the only single extracted from the original album release, entered the UK top twenty in December of that year.

"I Die: You Die" represented Numan at a creative crossroads, attempting to evolve his sound whilst maintaining the distinctive aesthetic that had brought him such remarkable success in the previous year.

The Britain of autumn 1980 was a markedly different place from the country that had first embraced Numan just over a year earlier. Margaret Thatcher's Conservative government, elected in May 1979, had begun implementing policies that would fundamentally reshape British society, though the full consequences of these changes were not yet entirely apparent.

Unemployment was rising sharply, industrial relations remained confrontational, and the optimism that had accompanied Thatcher's election was giving way to anxiety about the direction the country was taking. The social contract that had underpinned British society since the Second World War was being systematically dismantled, replaced by a vision of individualism and market forces that would prove deeply divisive. This was the context within which "I Die: You Die" appeared.

Musically, "I Die: You Die" represented both continuity with and evolution from Numan's earlier work. The track retained the synthesiser-based foundation, but there was a notable shift in both texture and mood. Where "Cars" had been built around a single, insistent hook that repeated throughout the track, "I Die: You Die" was more dynamically varied, featuring distinct sections that created a sense of progression and development. The production was denser, more layered, with multiple synthesiser parts weaving around each other to create a rich sonic tapestry.

Lyrically, "I Die: You Die" was targeted at and directed towards what Numan perceived and experienced as an increasingly vitriolic, hostile, and antagonistic music press. The track represented Numan's response to the mounting criticism and often savage treatment he was receiving from British music journalists, who had never been particularly sympathetic to his work and whose hostility had intensified considerably as his commercial success continued and expanded.

Numan's feelings of antagonism towards the music press were entirely understandable given the treatment he had endured from that quarter virtually from the outset of his career. The British music press of the late 1970s and early 1980s, particularly the influential weekly publications such as *New Musical Express* and *Sounds*, had established themselves as arbiters of taste and credibility within British popular music, wielding considerable power to make or break careers through their coverage and critical assessments.

By 1980, Numan had endured nearly two years of sustained critical hostility whilst simultaneously achieving remarkable commercial success. The song represented an opportunity to strike back, to articulate his frustration at critics who seemed determined to destroy him regardless of his achievements or the quality of his work.

The musical landscape into which "I Die: You Die" was released was characterised by considerable diversity and creative ferment. Synthesiser-based music had moved decisively into the mainstream in the year since "Cars" had topped the charts. Orchestral Manoeuvres in the Dark had achieved success with "Enola Gay," a track that shared some of Numan's electronic approach whilst bringing a more melodic, accessible quality. The Human League were beginning their transformation from avant-garde experimentalists into pop hitmakers, a process that would reach its apotheosis with "Don't You Want Me" the following year. Ultravox, with their new lead singer Midge Ure, were crafting a form of electronic rock that combined synthesisers with more traditional instrumentation.

What distinguished Numan's approach in "I Die: You Die" from much of this emerging synthesiser pop was its relative darkness and refusal to embrace more conventional pop sensibilities.

Where many of his contemporaries and successors were discovering ways to make electronic music brighter, more melodically immediate, more obviously radio-friendly, Numan remained committed to a vision that privileged atmosphere and mood over instant accessibility. There was a grandeur to "I Die: You Die," an almost gothic quality in its layered synthesisers and dramatic dynamics, that set it apart from the cleaner, more streamlined electronic pop that was gaining commercial traction.

Telekon represented the concluding studio album of what Numan would later retrospectively characterise and describe as the "Machine" section of his career. The album marked a significant shift in his sound, as it reintroduced guitar instrumentation to Numan's music after its notable absence on *The Pleasure Principle*, and also featured a broader and more diverse range of synthesiser models and sounds than his previous work had employed.

During the same year, Numan embarked upon his second major tour, which was given the title "The Teletour." This touring production featured a stage show that was considerably more elaborate and ambitious in its presentation than The Touring Principle tour that had taken place the previous year, demonstrating Numan's commitment to creating increasingly theatrical live experiences.

As 1980 was drawing to a close, On 17th December Numan was finally granted his pilot's licence. The following day he bought his first aeroplane for £12,000; a Cessna 182 Skylane.

In April 1981, Numan announced his decision to retire from touring altogether, stating that his forthcoming series of concerts at Wembley Arena would be his final live performances. These farewell concerts featured support from Nash the Slash, a Canadian experimental musician, and Shock, an unconventional performance troupe that combined elements of rock music, mime, and burlesque. The members of Shock included Barbie Wilde, the performance artists Tik and Tok, and Carole Caplin, who would later become known for other pursuits.

To coincide with these "farewell performances," a live two-album boxed set was released under the title *Living Ornaments '79 And '80*. This collection featured recordings from both his 1979 and 1980 tours and achieved considerable commercial

64

success, reaching number two in the UK charts. The two albums were also made available as separate individual releases, titled *Living Ornaments '79* and *Living Ornaments '80* and both of these standalone releases also achieved chart positions in their own right.

However, Numan's announced retirement from touring would prove to be short-lived, and he would soon reverse this decision and return to live performance, demonstrating that his connection to touring and direct audience engagement was stronger than he had initially believed.

Around this time on 1st July '81 the success he had attained was instrumental in helping Numan set up his own small charter flight company. Branding it as Numanair, it operated from Blackbushe Aerodrome in Surrey. The company acquired a Cessna 210 Centurion (registered G-OILS) and a Piper PA-31 Navajo (registered G-NMAN). He also indulged his passion for motor racing in 1981 by sponsoring Mike Mackonochie who drove a Van Diemen RF81 in Numanair livery in the Formula Ford 1600 class.

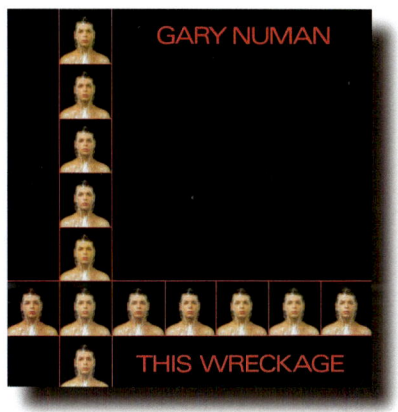

70

Boys Like Me

Moving away from the pure electropop sound with which he had become firmly associated and identified, Numan commenced a period of musical experimentation that saw him exploring jazz influences, funk rhythms, and a more ethereal, rhythmically focused approach to pop music. His first studio album following the farewell concerts he had performed at Wembley Arena was *Dance*, which appeared in 1981.

The album achieved the number three position on the UK album charts and remained on the charts for a total of eight weeks, demonstrating that Numan retained substantial commercial appeal despite his announced retirement from touring and his shift towards a different musical direction. The album generated one hit single, titled "She's Got Claws," which climbed to number six on the charts, providing further evidence of Numan's continued commercial viability even as he explored new sonic territories.

Dance was notable for featuring contributions from several distinguished and highly respected guest musicians from various established bands, representing a departure from Numan's usual practice of working primarily with his own backing band.

The album included performances by Mick Karn, who played both bass guitar and saxophone and was known for his work with the band Japan; guitarist Rob Dean, also from Japan; Roger Mason, a keyboard player from the Australian band Models; and Roger Taylor, the drummer from the legendary rock band Queen. This assembly of guest musicians from diverse musical backgrounds reflected Numan's desire to expand his sonic palette and bring different influences and textures into his evolving sound, moving beyond the purely synthesiser-based approach that had characterised his most commercially successful period.

Meanwhile, Numan's former backing band members—Chris Payne, who had played keyboards and viola, Russell Bell on guitar, and Ced Sharpley on drums—had regrouped and reformed themselves as a synth-pop band operating under the name Dramatis.

Numan maintained collaborative relationships with these former bandmates and contributed lead vocals

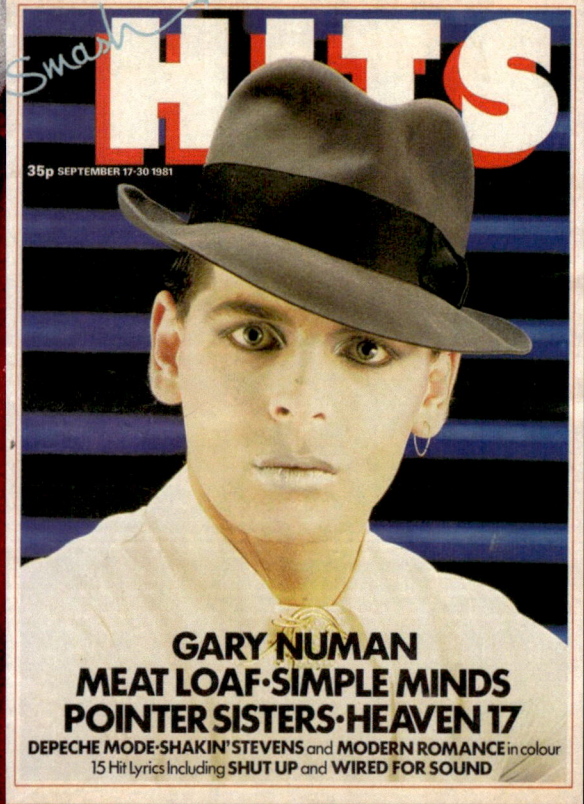

Smash HITS

35p October 2-15 1980

HIT LYRICS including
I Told You So
My Old Piano
Another One Bites The Dust

GARY NUMAN
BAD MANNERS
ROCKPILE

PAUL WELLER
ROBERT PALMER
in colour

A KORG SYNTHESIZER TO BE WON

Smash HITS

35p SEPTEMBER 17-30 1981

GARY NUMAN
MEAT LOAF·SIMPLE MINDS
POINTER SISTERS·HEAVEN 17
DEPECHE MODE·SHAKIN' STEVENS and MODERN ROMANCE in colour
15 Hit Lyrics Including SHUT UP and WIRED FOR SOUND

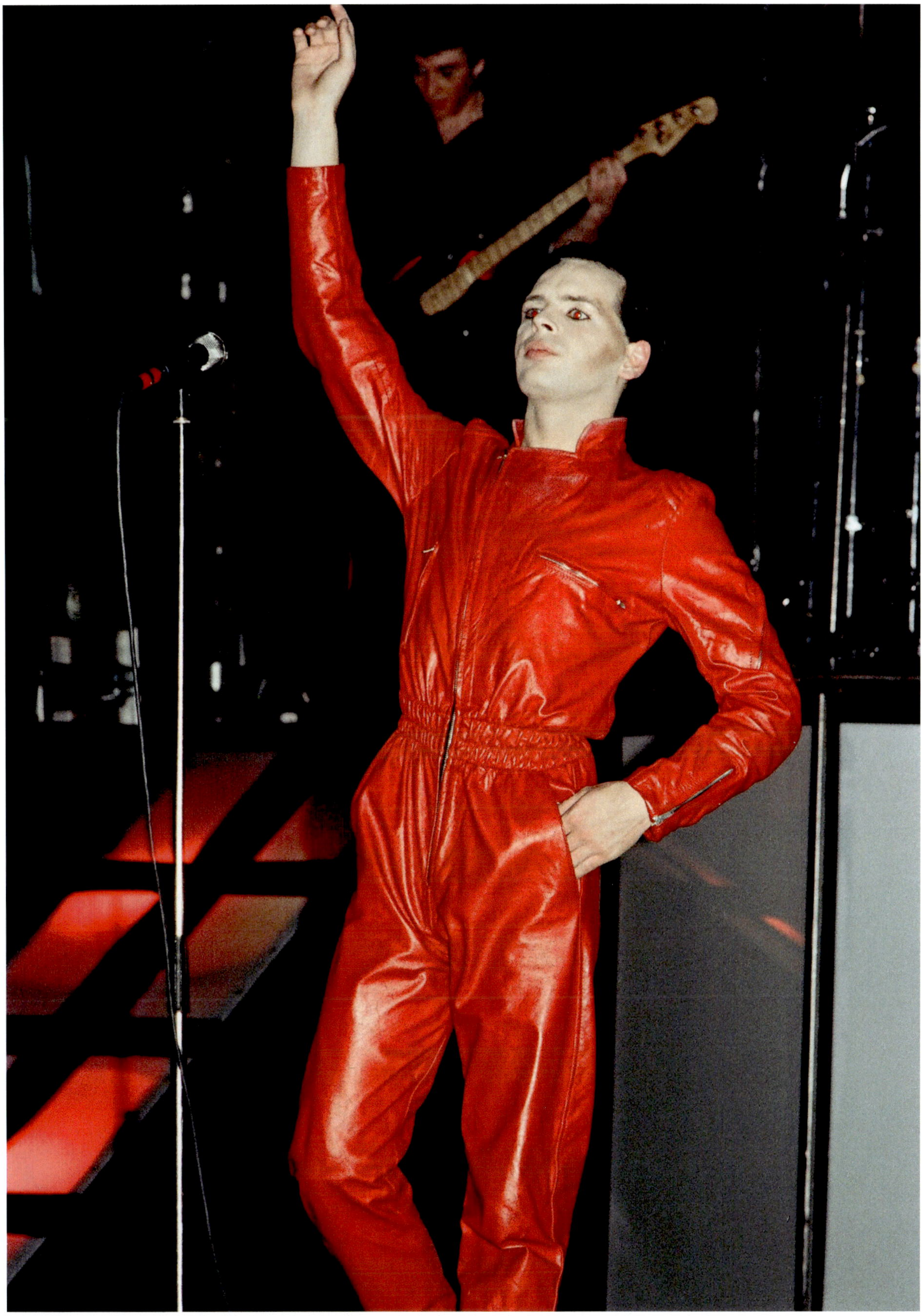

74

75

76

81

82

to their track "Love Needs No Disguise," which became a minor hit single and appeared on their 1981 studio album *For Future Reference*. Additionally, Numan lent his lead vocal talents to "Stormtrooper in Drag," the debut single released by Paul Gardiner, who had served as Numan's long-term bassist throughout much of his earlier success. This single also managed to achieve a chart position, demonstrating that Numan's name still carried commercial weight even when attached to other artists' projects.

However, despite these collaborative successes and his continued creative output, Numan's own commercial fortunes began to experience a decline as the 1980s progressed. He found himself being outsold in the marketplace by several acts who were working in similar electronic and synth-pop territories, including the Human League, who had successfully transitioned from experimental post-punk to mainstream pop success; Duran Duran, who were combining synthesisers with more traditional rock instrumentation and glamorous visual presentation; Depeche Mode, who were developing their own distinctive approach to electronic pop; and perhaps most tellingly, Orchestral Manoeuvres in the Dark (OMD), who had actually served as a support act on Numan's earlier tours but had now surpassed him in terms of commercial success and critical favour.

Numan continued to demonstrate considerable creative ambition and artistic restlessness, adopting a particular persona or character with each new studio album he released, using these different identities as frameworks for exploring various themes and musical directions. However, despite this ongoing commitment to reinvention and his refusal to simply repeat the formula that had brought him success, none of these subsequent personas and their accompanying albums succeeded in capturing the public's imagination or attention in the way he had so spectacularly managed to achieve in 1979, when his breakthrough had seemed to establish him as one of the defining artists of the new decade.

The magic that had made "Are 'Friends' Electric?" and "Cars" such cultural phenomena proved difficult to recapture, and Numan found himself in the increasingly frustrating position of being a pioneer whose innovations had opened doors through which others were now passing to greater commercial reward.

84

Outside of the music Gary and his co-pilot Bob Thompson set out to fly round the world in a Cessna 210 Centurion. Unfortunately, this first attempt came to an abrupt end on the sub-continent. On Saturday 26th September 1981 the *Shropshire Star* reported:

Pop star Gary Numan, reported to have been detained in India, said today: "It's the most frightening experience of my life." Gary and co-pilot Bob Thompson (36), today said they faced a third day of questioning by officials after their Cessna Centurion plane was forced to make an emergency landing at the east coast port of Visakhapatnam. Millionaire Gary (23), and father of three Bob, of Osmotherley, North Yorkshire, were on a round-the-world flight. When their aircraft engine faltered, they were forced to make their unscheduled touchdown on a civilian airstrip. Gary, who claimed he was due to face further questioning by security police, said from his hotel bedroom: "I feel rotten and fed up I have no idea how long I'm going to be detained.

"The authorities won't say exactly how long I will be detained. They make half-hearted accusations about spying or smuggling and wait to see what we say.

"They have confiscated all our film and sound recording equipment we were using to make a film of the journey, hopefully for television. They stripped our aircraft but I don't know what they are looking for."

He added "it was frightening when we had engine trouble out at sea. But this ordeal is worse. It's the most frightening experience of my life.

"We each have a plain clothes guard with us round the clock and are not allowed outside the hotel unless accompanied by guards."

The report continued by saying that Gary had not eaten for four days:

"I don't like Indian food," he said, and he described his hotel as "a hovel."

But Gary said: "We are determined to finish our round the world flight. Our aircraft is grounded with magneto problems.

"We hope eventually to get an engineer to it. But in the meantime we will have to return to London and rejoin our plane later."

The *Shropshire Star*, clearly keen on giving column inches to Numan also reported the following month on Thursday 8th October 1981:

Pop star Gary Numan appeared in court today, accused of possessing an

offensive weapon – a rounders bat. The 23-year-old millionaire, charged under his real name of Gary Anthony James Webb, should have attended Uxbridge magistrates court yesterday, but failed to surrender to bail, and an arrest warrant was issued. But today Mr Mark Cran, Numan's counsel, apologised for the pop star, who stood in the dock wearing a grey double-breasted suit and white shoes. Mr Cran said Numan's solicitors had written to the court asking yesterday's hearing to be adjourned. He said: "They thought because they had written it was not necessary for him to appear. "All I can do is offer apologies on their behalf. Mr Webb was told not to attend by his solicitors."

He asked for the case to be remanded as Numan was going on a five to six-week world tour, beginning on October 21. Mr Cran said the tour was scheduled for 44 days but might take longer because Mr Numan's private aircraft was impounded in southern India.

Magistrates' chairman Mrs Lavinia Cox remanded Numan on unconditional bail until December 21. Outside court Numan, of Wentworth, Surrey, signed autographs for several fans and said: "This just hasn't been my month. "First, I was held in India and now this. None of it

has been my fault. "I was very surprised when I heard the police had a warrant for my arrest, so I telephoned West Drayton police station last night and said I would be round today. The police were very nice and asked if I wanted a cup of tea. I refused, then they kindly escorted me to court later."

On Sunday 25th October Gary and Bob Thompson took off from Blackbushe Aerodrome in their second attempt to fly round the world. This time successfully in his Piper PA-31 Navajo, completing the trip in December.

****

Numan's fourth solo studio album, titled I, Assassin, was released in 1982 and demonstrated that he retained the ability to produce commercially successful singles even as his overall chart dominance had begun to diminish. The album generated a top ten hit with "We Take Mystery (To Bed)," which proved that Numan could still connect with mainstream audiences when the material was right. Additionally, two further singles extracted from the album—"Music For Chameleons" and "White Boys And Heroes"—both achieved top twenty chart positions,

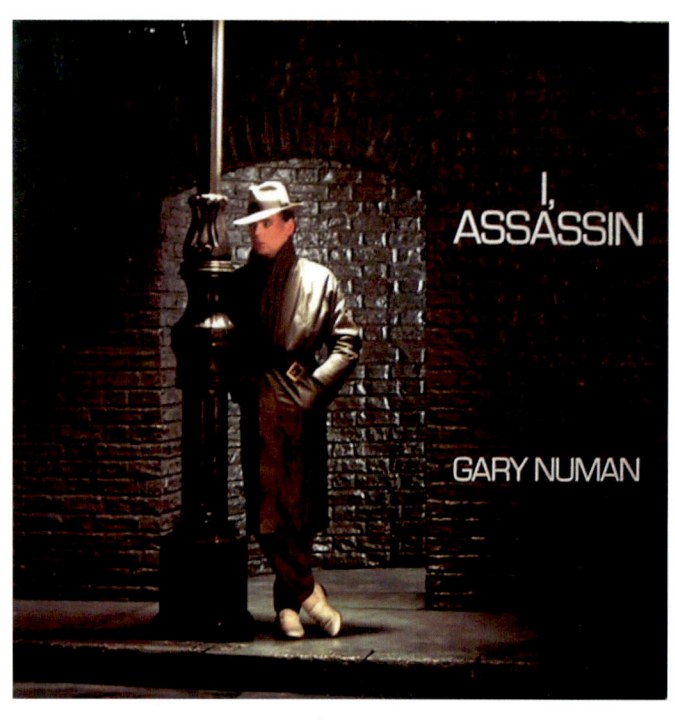

representing respectable if not spectacular commercial performances. The album itself peaked at number eight on the UK album charts and maintained a chart presence for six weeks, indicating solid if diminished commercial appeal compared to the chart-topping successes of his earlier releases.

The musical style of *I, Assassin* marked a significant departure from Numan's earlier synth-based sound, featuring a heavily percussive approach that incorporated substantial funk influences into his established electronic framework. This rhythmic emphasis proved particularly effective in certain contexts, and several tracks from the album found unexpected commercial success in markets and venues that had not previously been particularly receptive to Numan's work. Specifically, the twelve-inch extended version of "Music for Chameleons" and a specially created remix of "White Boys And Heroes" both became surprising successes within the American club scene, where their funk-influenced rhythms and danceable qualities appealed to audiences who might not otherwise have engaged with Numan's more experimental electronic work.

This unexpected American club success encouraged Numan to pursue opportunities in the United States more actively, and in October 1982 he embarked upon a tour of the US, attempting to capitalise on this newfound interest and to establish himself more firmly in the American market.

Warriors, released in 1983, represented a continuation and further development of the jazz-influenced musical style that Numan had begun exploring on previous releases. The album featured significant contributions from Bill Nelson, the avant-garde musician best known for his work with the band Be-Bop Deluxe. However, the collaboration between Numan and Nelson proved to be fraught with difficulties, and the two musicians experienced a falling out during the recording sessions. As a consequence of this dispute, Nelson made the decision to remove his name from the album's credits and chose to go uncredited despite having served as the album's co-producer, a decision that spoke to the severity of whatever disagreements had arisen between the two artists during the creative process.

93

94

The album also featured the talents of saxophonist Dick Morrissey, whose contributions added further jazz textures to Numan's evolving sound. Morrissey would maintain a working relationship with Numan beyond this album, going on to perform on several subsequent Numan releases including *The Fury*, *Strange Charm*, and *Outland*, establishing himself as a recurring collaborator during this particular phase of Numan's career.

Warriors achieved a peak chart position of number twelve on the UK album charts and produced two hit singles for Numan. The title track "Warriors" became one of these hits, reaching the top twenty and demonstrating that Numan could still generate commercially successful singles even as his albums were charting progressively lower than his earlier releases. Like its predecessor *I, Assassin*, *Warriors* maintained a presence on the album charts for six weeks, suggesting a consistent if somewhat diminished level of commercial appeal compared to the heights of 1979 and 1980.

The album held additional significance as it marked the end of Numan's association with Beggars Banquet Records, the independent label that had signed Tubeway Army and released all of Numan's work up to this point, including his breakthrough hits and most commercially successful releases. This departure from Beggars Banquet represented a significant moment in Numan's career, closing the chapter on the label relationship that had brought him to prominence.

Warriors was supported by an extensive touring schedule, with Numan undertaking a substantial forty-date tour of the UK to promote the album. Continuing a partnership he had established during his earlier farewell concerts, the tour once again featured support from Tik and Tok, the robotic mime and music duo whose distinctive performance style complemented Numan's own theatrical approach to live presentation. This extensive touring demonstrated Numan's continued commitment to live performance despite the commercial challenges he was facing, and his determination to maintain direct contact with the audience that had supported him throughout his career.

Following his departure from Beggars Banquet Records, Numan subsequently established and issued a series of albums and singles through his own independent record label, which he named Numa Records. This move towards complete independence gave him total creative control over his output but also meant he would be responsible for all aspects of distribution, promotion, and the business side of releasing records, areas where major labels typically provided substantial support and expertise.

The first studio album to be released through this new label arrangement was *Berserker*, which appeared in 1984. The album represented a significant technological shift in Numan's approach to music-making, marking his first substantial exploration and experimentation with music computers and sampling technology. Specifically, he employed the PPG Wave, a sophisticated digital synthesiser and sampler that represented the cutting edge of electronic music technology at the time, allowing him to create and manipulate sounds in ways that had not been possible with the analogue synthesisers that had characterised his earlier work.

The release of *Berserker* was accompanied by a comprehensive reinvention of Numan's visual identity and aesthetic presentation. He adopted a new colour scheme based around blue and white tones, which permeated all aspects of the album's presentation and his public image during this period. This visual transformation extended to Numan's own appearance, most strikingly manifested in his decision to dye his hair blue, creating a dramatic and eye-catching look that marked a clear break from his previous visual presentations. This new image was deployed across all promotional materials and performances associated with the album.

Numan supported the album's release with an extensive promotional campaign that included a tour to perform the new material live, a live album documenting performances from this tour, a video release capturing the visual aspects of the *Berserker* project, an extended play release, and the release of the title track "Berserker" as a single. This single achieved a respectable chart position, entering the UK top forty and suggesting that Numan still retained the ability to generate hit singles even if his album sales were becoming less reliable.

Despite this single success and the comprehensive promotional efforts surrounding the album, *Berserker* ultimately proved to be a disappointment both commercially and in terms of reception. The album divided opinion among both critics and Numan's

fanbase, with some appreciating the new technological direction whilst others felt he had lost the distinctive qualities that had made his earlier work compelling. This division of opinion was reflected in the album's commercial performance, which was distinctly poor by Numan's standards. The album stalled at number thirty-two on the UK album charts, representing his lowest chart position to date and a dramatic fall from the chart-topping successes he had enjoyed just a few years earlier.

Numan himself has offered numerous explanations for the album's commercial underperformance in subsequent interviews and reflections on this period of his career. Among the factors he has cited are significant distribution issues, which may have resulted from the challenges of operating through an independent label without the established distribution networks that major labels could provide. These distribution problems could have meant that the album was not available in sufficient quantities or in the right retail outlets at crucial moments, hampering its commercial potential regardless of its artistic merits. However, Numan has suggested that distribution was merely one among several factors that contributed to the album's disappointing reception and sales performance.

In 1984, away from the music, Numan bought a Harvard T-6 trainer aircraft registered G-AZSC and had the aircraft painted to resemble a Japanese "Zero" fighter. He also gained a display pilot's licence and flew the machine on the UK air display circuit. He and friend Norman Lees, who also owned a Harvard, formed the Radial Pair, and by 1992 they were performing synchronised aerobatics for the air display season. Later they teamed up with other Harvard owners to fly up to five aircraft as the Harvard Formation Team with Numan choreographing their aerobatic routines.

Numan also held licences for piston and turbine helicopters and had a fixed wing multi engine rating. He became an aerobatic flying instructor and was appointed by the Civil Aviation Authority (CAA) as an air display pilot evaluator such was his level of flying skill.

Back to the music and a collaborative project with Bill Sharpe, the keyboard player from the jazz-funk band Shakatak, proved to be considerably more successful than Numan's recent solo endeavours. The two musicians worked together under the joint billing of Sharpe & Numan, creating a partnership that combined their respective strengths and fan bases.

In March 1985, this collaboration yielded the single "Change Your Mind," which achieved a respectable chart performance by reaching number seventeen on the UK singles chart. This represented Numan's highest-charting single in some time and demonstrated that collaborative work might offer him opportunities for commercial success that were proving increasingly elusive in his solo career.

A few months following this collaborative success, Numan returned to releasing material under his own name with the live album *White Noise*. This release had been recorded during the Berserker Tour, capturing performances of material from that album alongside older favourites, and it provided fans with a document of Numan's live sound during this particular phase of his career. The album managed to achieve a chart position of number twenty-nine, a modest but respectable performance for a live album.

Additionally, a live extended play was extracted from the same concert recordings that had produced *White Noise*. This EP, which carried the straightforward title *The Live EP*, featured selected tracks taken from the full live album and was released as a separate product, presumably to provide a more accessible and affordable entry point for fans or to generate additional chart presence through a different format. *The Live EP* achieved a chart position

of number twenty-seven, performing slightly better than the full live album from which it was drawn, though both releases demonstrated that whilst Numan retained a dedicated fan base willing to purchase his releases, he was no longer commanding the chart dominance or mass audience appeal that had characterised his early career.

Numan's next studio album, *The Fury*, appeared in 1985 and achieved a chart performance that represented a modest improvement over the disappointing showing of *Berserker*. The album managed to break into the top thirty of the UK album charts, charting slightly higher than its predecessor and suggesting that Numan had at least arrested the decline in his commercial fortunes, even if he had not reversed it entirely.

In keeping with his established practice of adopting a new visual identity and aesthetic presentation with each album release, *The Fury* once again heralded a significant change of image for Numan. This time, he abandoned the blue hair and blue-and-white colour scheme that had characterised the *Berserker* era and instead presented himself in a markedly different style, appearing in promotional materials and performances wearing a white suit paired with a red bow tie. This sartorial

choice created a more formal, almost lounge-singer appearance that was quite different from any of his previous visual incarnations and suggested perhaps an attempt to position himself as a more mature, sophisticated artist.

However, despite the album's marginally improved chart performance and the fresh visual approach, *The Fury* marked a significant and troubling milestone in Numan's commercial decline. For the first time in his career since achieving fame, none of the three singles that were initially released from the album managed to penetrate the top forty of the UK singles chart. The three singles in question—"Your Fascination," "Call Out The Dogs," and "Miracles"— all performed disappointingly, barely scraping into the top fifty positions on the UK charts. This represented a dramatic fall from the days when Numan could reliably expect his singles to reach the top ten or even top the charts entirely, and it signalled that his commercial appeal had diminished substantially, that the mainstream audience that had once embraced his work so enthusiastically had largely moved on to other artists and sounds.

The failure of these singles to achieve significant chart success must have been particularly disheartening for Numan, as it suggested that even competent, professional work backed by promotional efforts and a new visual identity was no longer sufficient to guarantee commercial success in an increasingly crowded and competitive musical marketplace.

The following year brought some improvement to Numan's singles chart fortunes, with two releases managing to achieve top thirty positions in the UK charts. In April 1986, "This Is Love" was released and succeeded in reaching the top thirty, providing welcome evidence that Numan could still generate commercially viable singles. This was followed in June of that year by "I Can't Stop," which also achieved a top thirty chart position, suggesting that perhaps Numan's commercial decline might be stabilising and that he retained the ability to connect with a significant audience, at least in the singles format.

However, when the subsequent studio album *Strange Charm* was released later that same year, it told a rather different and considerably more disappointing story. Despite being preceded by two reasonably successful singles that might have been expected to generate interest in the parent album, *Strange Charm* performed extremely poorly on the album charts. The album managed only a brief two-week presence on the charts, a dramatic

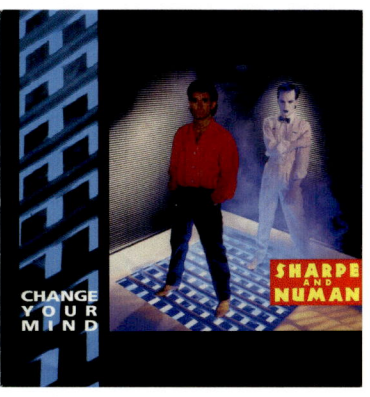

decline from the sustained chart runs his earlier albums had enjoyed, and it peaked at a lowly number fifty-nine.

This represented Numan's worst album chart performance to date and suggested a troubling disconnect between his ability to occasionally generate hit singles and his capacity to sell albums, indicating that whilst some listeners might be willing to purchase individual tracks, they were increasingly reluctant to invest in full-length albums of his material.

In November of that year, Numan released a version of the song "I Still Remember," a track that had originally appeared on *The Fury*, his previous studio album from the year before. This release was undertaken as a charity single, with proceeds going to the Royal Society for the Prevention of Cruelty to Animals (RSPCA). Despite the charitable nature of the release, which might have been expected to generate some goodwill and additional sales from fans willing to support a worthy cause, the single performed dismally on the charts.

It stalled at number seventy-four on the singles chart, failing to match the top thirty success of the two earlier singles from that year and reinforcing the sense that Numan's commercial fortunes remained highly unpredictable and that even recent successes could not be relied upon to predict future performance.

The poor showing of this charity single must have been particularly dispiriting with the cause being close to Gary's heart, and it suggested that even appealing to fans' charitable instincts and releasing material from what had been a reasonably well-received album could not guarantee commercial success in what were clearly difficult times for his career.

Further collaborative work with Bill Sharpe continued to yield results with the Sharpe & Numan partnership spawning two additional hit singles, though these achieved progressively more modest chart positions than their initial collaboration had managed. "New Thing From London Town" was released in 1986 and peaked at number fifty-two on the UK singles chart, representing a considerably lower chart position than "Change Your Mind" had achieved the previous year. This was followed in 1987 by "No More Lies," which performed somewhat better, reaching number thirty-five on the charts, though still falling short of the success their first collaboration had enjoyed. These releases demonstrated that whilst the Sharpe & Numan partnership retained some commercial viability, it was experiencing diminishing returns with

each successive release.

In 1987, Numan took on the role of lead vocalist for three singles released by Radio Heart, a musical project helmed by brothers Hugh and David Nicholson, who had previously been members of the bands Marmalade and Blue and brought his considerable experience to the project. These three singles achieved varying degrees of chart success, with none managing to break into the top thirty. The first single, "Radio Heart," performed best of the three, reaching number thirty-five on the UK charts. The second single, "London Times," achieved a more modest position, peaking at number forty-eight. The third single, "All Across the Nation," performed disappointingly, stalling at number eighty-one in the UK, barely registering on the charts at all.

A full studio album was also released as part of the Radio Heart project, credited to "Radio Heart featuring Gary Numan" in recognition of his participation and presumably to capitalise on his name recognition. However, Numan's involvement in the album was actually quite limited, with him appearing as vocalist on only three tracks out of the album's full track listing. That didn't stop the label having Gary as the cover photo.

The album also included Elton John whose name was also on the front cover. Despite the prominent use of their names in the billing, which might have been expected to generate some commercial interest, the record failed entirely to achieve any chart position, suggesting that by this point Numan's name alone was insufficient to guarantee even modest commercial success for projects with which he was associated.

Also, during 1987, Numan's former label, Beggars Banquet Records, with whom he had parted ways several years earlier, released a double disc compilation album titled *Exhibition*. This retrospective collection drew from Numan's catalogue of work released through the label during his most commercially successful period and managed to achieve a chart position of number forty-three on the UK Albums Chart. Whilst this was far from a spectacular performance, it demonstrated that there remained sufficient interest in Numan's earlier work to generate respectable sales for a compilation release, even if his new material was struggling to find an audience.

Beggars Banquet also released a newly created remix of "Cars." This remix was given the title "Cars (E Reg Model)," a playful reference to the UK vehicle registration system which used

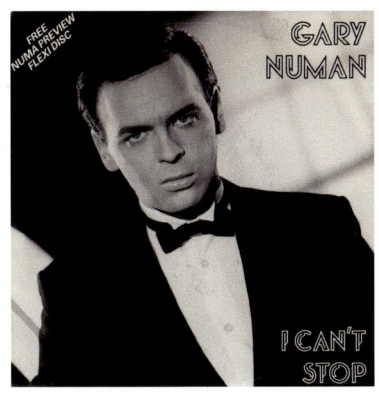

letter prefixes to indicate the year of a car's manufacture, with 'E Reg' denoting vehicles registered in 1987-88.

The remix proved considerably more successful than most of Numan's recent original material, charting at number sixteen on the UK singles chart. This achievement marked a significant milestone, as it represented Numan's final top twenty hit single, at least until the same song would be re-released once again in 1996, nearly a decade later.

The success of this remix compared to his new material must have presented Numan with a bittersweet situation—whilst it was gratifying to see one of his songs back in the charts, the fact that only a reworking of eight-year-old material could achieve significant commercial success whilst his new work languished underlined how far his commercial fortunes had fallen and how difficult he was finding it to connect with contemporary audiences with fresh material.

Numa Records, the independent record label that Numan had established and launched during a period of idealistic excitement and optimism about the possibilities of complete creative and business independence, was forced to fold and cease operations following the release of *Strange Charm*, Numan's eighth solo studio album, in 1986.

The label's closure represented the failure of Numan's attempt to control all aspects of his career through complete independence, demonstrating that the challenges of distribution, promotion, and the business side of running a record label had ultimately proved insurmountable despite his best efforts and intentions.

The commercial failure of Numa Records was not an isolated financial setback but formed part of a broader and more devastating pattern of financial decline that saw Numan's personal wealth dramatically eroded during this period. The considerable fortune he had amassed since the late 1970s through his enormous commercial success—which he estimated to have been approximately £4.5 million at its peak, a very substantial sum representing the rewards of multiple number one albums and singles—was completely drained away.

This catastrophic loss of wealth, accumulated over less than a decade of unprecedented success, must have been psychologically devastating as well as financially ruinous, representing not merely a return to his pre-fame economic status but the squandering of years of commercial success and the security that wealth might have provided.

Faced with these dire financial circumstances and the collapse of his own label, Numan found himself in need of a recording contract with an established label that could provide the distribution, promotion, and financial support his own label had failed to deliver. He signed a recording contract with I.R.S. Records, an independent label founded by Miles Copeland III and associated with artists like R.E.M. and The Go-Go's, for the release of what would prove to be his final studio album of the 1980s.

This album, titled *Metal Rhythm*, appeared in 1988 and continued Numan's pattern of commercial underperformance, selling relatively poorly and failing to reverse his declining commercial fortunes. The album represented another disappointment in what had become a long series of commercial failures, each one further eroding Numan's position in the marketplace and his confidence in his ability to connect with contemporary audiences.

For the American release of *Metal Rhythm*, I.R.S. Records made a series of changes to the album that were implemented against Numan's wishes, demonstrating the loss of creative control that came with signing to an established label after the complete independence he had enjoyed with Numa Records. The record label edited and changed the album's title from *Metal Rhythm* to *New Anger*, taking the title from the album's lead single in what was presumably an attempt to make the release more marketable or accessible to American audiences. Additionally, they altered the album cover's colour scheme, changing it from black to blue, presumably for similar commercial or aesthetic reasons. Most significantly from a musical standpoint, the label remixed several of the album's tracks, altering the sound and production that Numan had crafted in ways he did not approve of or agree with.

These changes, implemented without Numan's consent or approval, must have been particularly galling given that they were being imposed by a label he had signed with out of financial necessity rather than artistic sympathy. The experience demonstrated the difficult position Numan found himself in—lacking the financial resources to maintain independence through his own label, he was forced to sign with established labels who felt entitled to override his artistic decisions in pursuit of commercial considerations, resulting in releases that did not represent his vision, but which bore his name nonetheless.

GARY NUMAN

● He's had a hair transplant, flown his own plane around the world and been threatened with death for his "wild sex romps". ● He believes in marriage, would like to have children and thinks people who put down the Royal Family should be shot. ● He's got a wolf in his living room, an eight foot teddy bear in his dining room and a "reporter" in his hall. . .

If you'd met me two weeks ago," beams Gary Numan, snuggling into a comfy armchair in his living room, "I wouldn't have been so happy. I'd just had three fairly duff singles and. . ."

And things weren't going very well at all. Seven years ago, back in the days when he had a group called Tubeway Army, Gary lurched into the charts with a record called "Are Friends Electric?" That song, a pleasant little synthesiser tune over which he spoke and "sung" in his distinctive steely voice, went to number one and for a long time afterwards he could do no wrong. But by the beginning of the '80s it had begun to slip and by last year Gary couldn't get his records even near the top ten.

"I really thought that was it," he recalls. "At the end of last year I began to seriously think about what else I could do." But he resolved to give it at least one more try, wrote a dreamy ballad called "This Is Love" and – hey presto! – he's back.

Which is why he's positively bubbling with pleasure this morning. Everything seems to be going right. His fan club, full of incredibly loyal followers who kept him going during the "lean years," has recently swollen to 3,500 members (as organiser, Gary's mum Beryl, will testify). His record company, Numa Records, which is run by his father, and into which Gary sunk all his money, finally looks like tasting success. And to cap it all he's in love – his girlfriend, Tracey Adams (referred to in the "news"papers as a "sexy vicar's daughter") has been living with Gary for the last year. In fact, there's only one or two little things that make life anything less than perfect. . .

"It's a shame," says Gary, "about the death threats. My mum got another one yesterday." *Death threats??!* "Yeah," answers Gary nonchalantly. "Letters. . .phone calls. . .I remember one bloke said he was going to kill me when I played at Wembley but he said 'I was enjoying it so much I decided to do it later'. And for every one that wants to kill you, there's three or four who want to cut you up or kill your dogs." But thankfully, nothing has actually happened. . .yet.

"One day we moved the car out of the garage and there were two milk bottles full of petrol underneath. Apparently that was to frighten us," explains Gary. That one, he says, was from someone who claimed Gary was a pervert after reading a story in a "news"paper about Gary's "wild sex romps". Which presumably weren't true in the first place? "A bit true maybe," says Gary. "Being sort of young and impressionable

▲ "This is a genuine Alaskan timber wolf. Yes, it *is* dead. I saw it in Seattle airport in America – it cost £1,000. I know it sounds a bit hypocritical but I'm actually all for this anti-fur campaign going on – the thing is, it was dead already and at the airport there were all these kids hanging on it and crawling all over it. I thought that was disgusting so I thought I'd buy it and give it a good home."

I got sucked into it now and again – the rock'n'roll thing, the wild women. It seemed great at the time though once you've done it a bit the novelty sort of wears off."

Fame came as a bit of a shock to Gary as a wide-eyed 21-year-old who'd spent his youth "reading all the Biggles books", joining the air cadets at 13 and alternatively dreaming of being a pilot and "miming in front of the mirror and having bedroom bands that were going to rule the world". He remembers his last holiday back in 1979, so disastrous that he's never been away since. . .

"It was dreadful. I'd just got famous and I said 'Cor. Look at all this money. I'm going to go on holiday'. So me and my mate Chris went down to Weymouth. Now when I was growing up, if you had a lot of money you had a six berth caravan at Littlesea Holiday Park and if you didn't you had a tourer. I didn't dream about hotels. . .skiing, St Tropez! I just got a six berth caravan and I thought I was *rolling* in it! And 'Are Friends Electric?' was number one so we got besieged and spent the whole week in there with the curtain shut. I was so naive."

And, after that, misadventures of one sort or another seemed to follow with depressing regularity.

He was blackmailed by a "lover" ("we got out of it by getting something on *her*," he reveals sinisterly), ridiculed in the streets ("I don't go out shopping or anything – there's a few people who take great delight in telling you they'd don't like you and there's a few who want to *show* you how much they don't like you. . ."), ridiculed even more for

flying round the world (something he's understandably still *very* upset about: "I thought people would be *proud* of me") and, to cap it all, his hair fell out. The last, at least, he managed to reverse a couple of years back – at a price.

"I had two operations," he explains enthusiastically, "both of them *unbelievably* painful. But it was worth it. If I'd have been a dustman I'd have done it – it was just one hundred per cent vanity. I didn't want to be bald." And having gone through it he seems to *love* recounting the gory details.

"I've got 206 stitches in my head – the first operation was 96 and the second 110. The actual operation doesn't hurt that much, it's the three or four days afterwards. The anaesthetic for the stitches swirls down your face and your face puffs up and all the stitches rip out. . ."

That's quite enough of *that*, thank you. Time to move on to some more wholesome subjects like, um, being nice to people. . .

"I don't believe in the goodness of man," states Gary matter-of-factly.

Oh.

"I believe that, deep down, man is a real shit. If there weren't any laws and I didn't know I'd get put inside, there's quite a few people I'd have tried to 'take out'. . ."

Eeek! That's quite enough about murdering people, *thank you*. . .

Despite all this talk of "blackmail" and "taking out" people, Gary comes across as a quiet, friendly sort of bloke who doesn't drink ("I've never been drunk in my life"), thinks the world of the Royal Family ("people who put them

down should be shot"), believes in marriage ("I've been brought up to think that you get married and you *stay* married"), wants children ("a couple – I've never really thought why. It just appeals to me, having a little boy and teaching him things") and, most of all, doesn't believe in mincing his words. Which is why he gets so hot under the collar about being labelled by more left wing groups as a money-grabbing capitalist. "I'm pointed out as the bad boy!" he explodes, "and yet *I'm* the one losing a hundred thousand pounds a tour giving money back to the fans. I really resent that."

It's "the fans" most of all who Gary worries about. Time and time again he gets in a fury about anyone who he thinks "rips them off", and he constantly refers to them as the people who put him where he is today. He explains that it's for the fans that he changes his "image" every year – "the white face and blue hair", the warrior, the space cadet, the "cheap Buck Rogers." The new image (which he's not sporting today) is his "Clark Gable rip-off" ("I was looking through an old book of Hollywood heroes and I wanted an image with a dicky-bow. It's my man at the casino image – I thought I should stop looking like a hyped-up young teenage rock'n'roll star.")

It's also for his fans that he does strange things like his next project, a set of about ten 90 minute long "interview albums".

"I thought it would be a fairly novel way of doing an autobiography," says Gary. He doesn't expect many people to buy it but says it's his chance once and for all to put across *his* side of all the things that have been said about him. And, in any case, "if nothing else it'll be nice for me when I'm grey and old to look back."

Because, he explains, he doesn't expect anyone else to even remember who Gary Numan is by then.

"I'd be a quite happy to be 30 and forgotten," he insists. "I don't *want* to be remembered and I don't think what I do is particularly *worthy* of being remembered anyway. I never thought that 'Are Friends Electric?' was a particularly great song. I find it a little *embarrassing* that people like me are considered heroes. What I do isn't particularly clever and certainly isn't brave – I've always associated heroes with being brave.

"If you say Douglas Bader (*famous World War II flying "ace" with no legs*) was a hero," Gary says reverentially, "and then *I'm* a hero then that's just one hundred percent embarrassing. It's a million miles apart. He *was* a hero – I'm just lucky."

● **Interview: Chris Heath** ● **Photos: Mike Putland**

Welcome To Love

In 1989, the Sharpe & Numan partnership, which had previously generated several moderately successful singles, released their first and only full-length studio album together, titled *Automatic*. This release came through Polydor Records, a major label, which might have been expected to provide the kind of distribution and promotional support that could help the album achieve commercial success. However, despite whatever advantages the major label backing might have provided, the album failed entirely to garner much commercial success or make any significant impact on the charts.

Automatic's chart performance was dismal even by the standards of Numan's recent struggles. The album managed to enter the UK album charts for just a single week, achieving a peak position of number fifty-nine before disappearing entirely from the charts. This represented a particularly poor showing, charting eleven positions lower than *Metal Rhythm*, which had been released nine months earlier. The fact that a collaborative album released through a major label performed worse than a solo album that had itself been considered a commercial disappointment underscored just how difficult the commercial climate had become for Numan and projects associated with him.

Only one single was extracted and released from *Automatic*. The track, titled "I'm On Automatic," was presumably chosen as the most commercially viable song from the album, the one most likely to generate radio play and chart success. However, it too performed disappointingly, reaching only number forty-four on the UK singles chart. This represented a significant step down from the chart positions that earlier Sharpe & Numan collaborations had achieved and suggested that whatever commercial appeal the partnership had once possessed had largely dissipated.

The poor sales performance of both *Automatic* and its sole single had immediate and significant consequences for the Sharpe & Numan collaboration. Plans that had apparently been in development for a second studio album were abandoned entirely in the wake of *Automatic's* commercial failure. The decision to cancel these plans demonstrated that whatever enthusiasm had existed for continuing the partnership had evaporated in the face of commercial reality. Neither artist nor their record label could justify investing further time, effort, and resources into a collaboration that had proven unable to generate significant sales or chart success, and the Sharpe & Numan project was effectively brought to an end, with the two musicians going their separate ways professionally.

In 1991, Numan expanded his creative activities beyond recording albums and performing, venturing into the field of film scoring when he collaborated with composer Michael R. Smith to co-compose the musical score for *The Unborn*, an American science fiction horror film. This represented Numan's first significant work in film composition and demonstrated his willingness to explore new creative territories and apply his skills in electronic music to the different demands and constraints of scoring for cinema. The musical score they created for the film would eventually receive a commercial release in 1995 as an album titled *Human*, allowing fans and interested listeners to experience the soundtrack work outside the context of the film itself.

Following this foray into film scoring, Numan returned to recording albums under his own name with *Outland*, which appeared in 1991. This album represented his second and what would prove to be his final studio album released through I.R.S. Records, bringing to an end a label relationship that had not proven particularly fruitful for either party.

Outland continued Numan's pattern of producing work that satisfied neither critics nor the record-buying public, representing another critical and commercial disappointment in what had become a dispiriting succession of failures. The album's poor reception effectively ended his relationship with I.R.S. Records and left him once again in need of a label through which to release his music.

In response to this situation, Numan made the decision to reactivate Numa Records, the independent label he had established in the mid-1980s and subsequently shut following a series of commercial disappointments. This second incarnation of Numa Records would serve as the release vehicle for his next two studio albums, representing another attempt at maintaining creative independence despite the financial and commercial challenges such independence entailed.

The first release under the reactivated Numa Records was *Machine + Soul*, which appeared in 1992. This album occupies a particularly unfortunate position in Numan's discography, being considered by many observers, critics, and fans—and indeed by Numan himself in subsequent reflections on his career—to represent a career low point, perhaps the nadir of his creative and commercial trajectory.

The circumstances surrounding the album's creation and release were particularly dispiriting, as it was released primarily not out of artistic conviction or creative inspiration but out of financial necessity, specifically to generate income that could be used to pay off the substantial debts Numan had accumulated during his years of commercial decline and the failure of his various business ventures. Creating work primarily to service debt rather than to express artistic vision represented a humiliating position for an artist who had once topped the charts and enjoyed complete creative freedom.

The reception accorded to *Machine + Soul* was predictably poor, with the album failing to achieve either critical acclaim or commercial success, confirming that work created primarily out of financial desperation rather than artistic conviction was unlikely to connect with audiences or generate the kind of positive response that might have helped reverse Numan's commercial fortunes.

Following the poor reception and disappointing sales of this album, Numan reached what appears to have been a crisis point in his career and his relationship with music-making. He seriously considered leaving the music industry entirely, abandoning the career that had once brought him such spectacular success, but which had become a source primarily of disappointment, debt, and diminishing returns. That he was contemplating retirement from music in his mid-thirties, having achieved fame less than fifteen years earlier, speaks to the depth of the difficulties he was experiencing and the extent to which his confidence had been eroded by years of commercial failure and critical dismissal.

In 1993, Numan made another attempt to capitalise on his past glories by releasing a single titled "Cars ('93 Sprint)," a techno remix of "Cars." This represented yet another return to that well, another attempt to extract commercial value from the one song that audiences consistently responded to, reimagined through the contemporary production techniques and musical styles of the early 1990s when techno and electronic dance music were enjoying mainstream popularity. The decision to release yet another version of "Cars" suggested both the enduring power of that particular composition and the difficulty Numan was experiencing in creating new material that could generate comparable interest.

During that same year, in what must have represented a particularly pointed reversal of fortunes, Numan accepted a position as support act on a concert tour headlined by Orchestral Manoeuvres in the Dark (OMD).

By 1994, Numan arrived at a crucial decision regarding the future direction of his career and creative work. He resolved to abandon his efforts to crack the pop market, to stop attempting to chase commercial success by trying to adapt his sound to whatever seemed commercially viable at any given moment. Instead, he determined to concentrate his energies on exploring more personal themes in his music, including subjects that were deeply meaningful to him personally rather than calculated to achieve radio play or chart success.

Among these personal themes was his vocal atheism, a subject he had occasionally touched upon or explored in previous studio albums but which he now felt free to address more directly and substantially without worrying about whether such material would alienate potential audiences or radio programmers.

This artistic reorientation was significantly encouraged and supported by Gemma O'Neill, a member of his fan club from Sidcup in south-east London. She would later become his wife. She played an important role in helping him find his way back to a more authentic creative voice by encouraging him to strip away the various musical influences and stylistic experiments of the more recent years, all the attempts to adapt to changing fashions and contemporary trends that had characterised his work through the late 1980s and early 1990s.

O'Neill's encouragement helped Numan recognise that his attempts to remain commercially relevant by incorporating whatever seemed fashionable had actually distanced him from the qualities that had made his best work compelling, and that a return to a more personal, less calculated approach might offer a way forward both artistically and potentially commercially.

Numan thus sought to achieve a grittier, more aggressive, and notably more industrial tone for his songwriting on what would become his twelfth solo studio album, *Sacrifice*. This shift towards industrial sounds and textures represented both a new direction and, in some ways, a return to the darker, more uncompromising qualities of his earliest work.

Significantly, Numan chose to play

almost all the instruments himself on *Sacrifice*, marking the first time in his career he had taken on such comprehensive instrumental duties. This decision to handle the instrumentation personally rather than employing session musicians or a backing band allowed him complete control over the album's sound and direction, ensuring that the final product represented his vision without compromise or dilution.

The timing of this shift towards a darker, more industrial sound proved fortuitous, as the musical landscape was changing in ways that would prove favourable to his new direction.

Nine Inch Nails, an American industrial rock project led by Trent Reznor, had been significantly influenced by Numan's music, particularly his earlier, darker work, and they were contemporaneously becoming famous and achieving substantial commercial success. Other bands working with industrial tendencies and exploring similar sonic territories were also gaining prominence and critical attention during this same period, suggesting that the cultural moment might finally be catching up with aspects of Numan's artistic vision that had seemed ahead of their time or commercially unviable when he had first explored them.

Sacrifice, when it was released, received critical acclaim, representing a dramatic reversal of the pattern of critical dismissal and hostility that had characterised responses to Numan's work for much of the previous decade and a half. Critics who had long dismissed his work or ignored it entirely now found much to praise in *Sacrifice*, recognising in it a renewed artistic conviction and a sound that connected with contemporary trends whilst maintaining Numan's distinctive voice and vision.

According to Numan himself, the influence between his work and that of Nine Inch Nails was mutual rather than simply flowing in one direction. Whilst Nine Inch Nails had clearly been influenced by Numan's pioneering electronic and industrial work from the late 1970s and early 1980s, Numan acknowledged that Nine Inch Nails' success and their approach to industrial rock had in turn influenced his own thinking about where he might take his music.

This mutual influence represented a satisfying validation for Numan—artists who had been inspired by his work were now achieving the kind of success that had eluded him for years, and their success was in turn helping to create a cultural climate in which his own work could find renewed appreciation.

Numan has been quite specific about his admiration for Nine Inch Nails' work, citing particular tracks that he finds especially compelling. He has identified the 1994 track "Closer" as his favourite Nine Inch Nails song, praising its combination of aggressive industrial sonics with commercially viable songwriting.

Additionally, he has expressed particular admiration for "Head Like A Hole," which appeared on Nine Inch Nails' 1989 debut album *Pretty Hate Machine*, going so far as to say that it features "the best chorus ever," an emphatic statement of appreciation that demonstrates the depth of his regard for Trent Reznor's songwriting abilities.

Beyond Nine Inch Nails, another significant influence on the sound and direction of *Sacrifice* came from Depeche Mode, the British electronic band who had themselves been influenced by Numan's early work and had gone on to achieve sustained commercial success throughout the 1980s and into the 1990s.

Specifically, Depeche Mode's eighth studio album, *Songs Of Faith And Devotion*, which was released in 1993 whilst Numan was in the process of recording *Sacrifice*, became a massive and transformative influence on his work. The album's combination of electronic textures with darker, more introspective lyrical themes, its exploration of spiritual and existential questions, and its generally sombre and serious tone both musically and lyrically provided inspiration for Numan's own new, darker direction.

Songs Of Faith And Devotion demonstrated that electronic music could be both commercially successful and artistically serious, that it could address weighty themes without sacrificing sonic innovation, and this example helped embolden Numan to pursue his own vision for a darker, more personal body of work without worrying excessively about whether such an approach could find commercial success.

A Question Of Faith

Sacrifice represented and marked the final studio album that Numan would create and release before making the decision to shut down Numa Records permanently, bringing a definitive end to his experiments with operating his own independent record label. After two separate attempts at running Numa Records, first in the mid-1980s and then again in the early 1990s, Numan evidently concluded that the challenges of maintaining an independent label—the distribution difficulties, the financial pressures, the lack of promotional resources that major labels could provide—made it unsustainable, and he closed down the operation for good.

His next two studio albums, *Exile* which appeared in 1997 and *Pure* which followed in 2000, were both released on Eagle Records, a growing independent label. These albums proved to be significant both artistically and in terms of Numan's critical rehabilitation. Both were well received by critics and

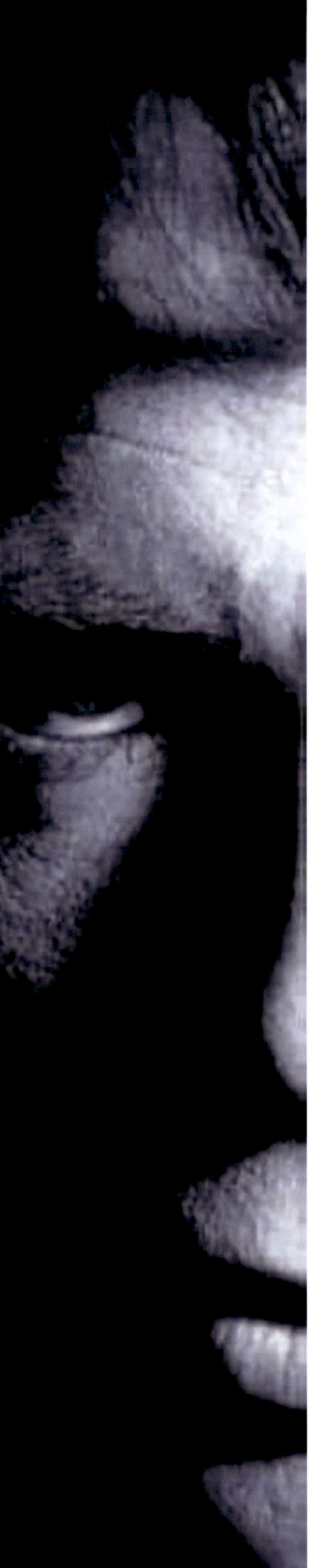

audiences, representing a dramatic improvement over the dismissive or hostile reception that had greeted much of his work throughout the late 1980s and early 1990s.

The positive response to these albums significantly helped to restore Numan's critical reputation, demonstrating that the artistic renewal evidenced on *Sacrifice* had not been a one-off occurrence but represented a genuine creative renaissance, a return to form that suggested Numan remained a vital and relevant artistic voice despite the years of commercial and critical wilderness he had endured.

The restoration of Numan's critical standing was further aided and accelerated by the release of *Random*, a double-CD tribute album dedicated to Numan's music and influence, which appeared in 1997. The timing of *Random's* release was particularly significant, as it came out shortly before *Exile*, helping to create a cultural context and renewed interest in Numan's work that would benefit the reception of his new album. The tribute album served multiple important functions: it demonstrated the breadth and depth of Numan's influence on subsequent generations of musicians, it reminded critics and audiences of his pioneering role in electronic music, and it associated him with contemporary artists who were themselves commercially successful and critically respected, thereby lending him some of their cultural capital and credibility.

The artist roster featured on *Random* was particularly impressive and telling, including contributions from prominent and commercially successful acts who openly acknowledged having been influenced by Numan's work. Among the participating artists were Damon Albarn, the frontman of Blur, one of the most successful and critically acclaimed British bands of the 1990s; EMF, who had achieved international success with their indie-dance crossover sound; Jesus Jones, another successful British alternative rock band; The Orb, pioneering figures in ambient house and electronic music; Moloko, the trip-hop and electronic duo; and Pop Will Eat Itself, an industrial rock band whose aggressive electronic sound owed clear debts to Numan's innovations.

The participation of such a diverse array of successful contemporary artists, spanning multiple genres but all united in their acknowledgment of Numan's influence, provided powerful evidence that his work had been far more influential and significant than the critical dismissals of the 1980s had suggested.

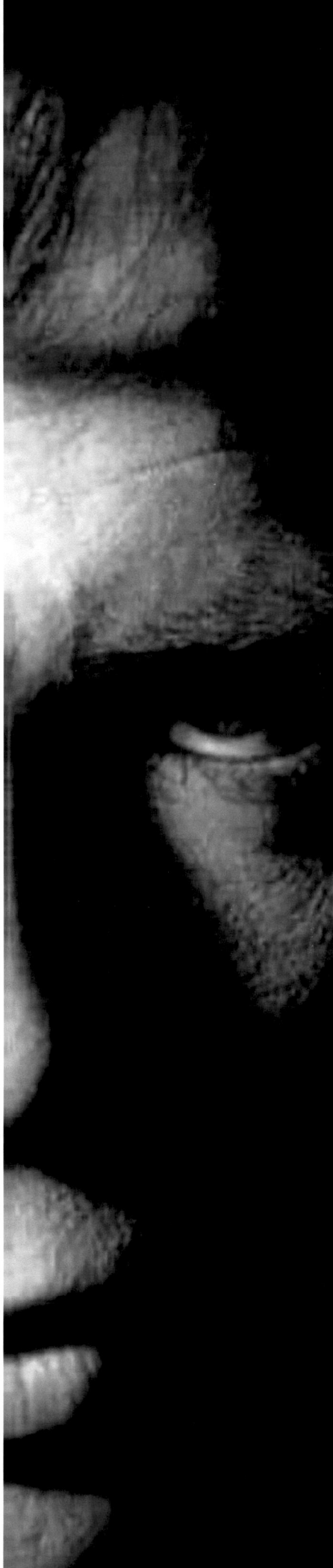

The tribute album format itself represented a form of validation and recognition that had important implications for how Numan was perceived. Tribute albums are typically reserved for artists whose influence and importance are widely recognised, whose catalogues are considered sufficiently substantial and significant to warrant reinterpretation by other artists.

That an array of successful contemporary musicians were willing to contribute their time and creative efforts to reinterpreting Numan's work signalled that he was increasingly being recognised not as a has-been or a novelty act from the late 1970s, but as an important and influential figure in the history of electronic music whose innovations had shaped the work of multiple subsequent generations of artists.

Building on the momentum created by the tribute album and the positive reception for *Exile*, Gary undertook a tour of the United States in support of the album. This represented his first series of concerts in America since the early 1980s, marking a return to a market he had largely abandoned or been forced to abandon during his years of commercial difficulty.

The decision to tour the US after such a long absence demonstrated renewed confidence in his work and his ability to connect with audiences, as well as recognition that there existed American audiences interested in his music, whether longtime fans who had followed his career through its difficulties or younger listeners who had discovered his work through the artists he had influenced.

The US tour represented both a practical effort to promote *Exile* and a symbolic statement that Numan was once again a viable touring artist capable of attracting audiences internationally, not merely in the UK where he retained a core following even during his most difficult years.

In 2002, Gary experienced a welcome return to chart success after years of struggling to achieve significant chart positions with his new material. The single "Rip" was released and managed to reach number twenty-nine on the UK singles chart, representing his highest chart position for a new single in many years and demonstrating that he had regained the ability to connect with contemporary audiences and achieve mainstream chart success rather than merely appealing to a dedicated cult following.

This chart success continued and indeed improved the following year, 2003, with the release of "Crazier," a collaborative single credited to Gary Numan vs Rico. Rico was a producer and remixer who had become an important collaborator during this period of Numan's career, helping him to update his sound and connect with contemporary electronic music trends.

"Crazier" achieved an even more impressive chart performance than "Rip" had managed, reaching number thirteen on the UK charts–Numan's highest chart position for new material since the mid-1980s and provided compelling evidence that his critical and commercial rehabilitation was translating into genuine mainstream success rather than merely improved reviews and cult appreciation.

Rico's collaboration with Numan extended beyond individual singles to encompass more substantial projects. He worked extensively on *Hybrid*, a remix album released in 2003 that featured comprehensive reworkings of older songs from Numan's catalogue. These tracks were reimagined and reconstructed in a more contemporary industrial style that reflected current trends in electronic music whilst maintaining the essential qualities that had made the original versions compelling. The album did not consist entirely of remixed older material, however, as it also included new

material created specifically for this release, blending retrospective and contemporary approaches.

The *Hybrid* album represented a collaborative effort that went well beyond simply Rico's contributions, featuring work from an impressive array of other artists and producers who each brought their own distinctive approaches to reimagining Numan's material.

Among those who contributed remixes were Curve, the alternative rock band known for their heavy, guitar-driven sound combined with electronic elements; Flood, one of the most respected and successful producers in alternative and electronic music, known for his work with acts like Nine Inch Nails, Depeche Mode, and U2; Andy Gray, a producer and engineer with extensive experience in electronic music; Alan Moulder, another highly regarded producer and engineer who had worked with numerous successful alternative and electronic acts; New Disease, who brought their own industrial sensibilities to the project; and Sulpher, an industrial rock band whose aggressive electronic sound aligned well with Numan's new direction.

This diverse array of contributors ensured that *Hybrid* offered multiple perspectives on Numan's catalogue, each remix reflecting different aspects of his influence and different ways his work could be reinterpreted for contemporary audiences.

Also in 2003, Numan expanded his collaborative activities by performing the lead vocals on "Pray for You," a track that served as the single from *Eargasm*, the second studio album by Plump DJs, a British duo known for their work in breakbeat and electronic dance music. This collaboration demonstrated Numan's willingness to work across different electronic genres and with artists from different scenes within electronic music.

The single achieved a modest chart position, reaching number eighty-nine on the UK Top 100 Chart, which whilst not representing a major hit nonetheless indicated that Numan's voice and presence could still add value to other artists' projects and help them achieve chart recognition.

In 2005, Gary made another significant business decision by choosing to take control of his own business affairs once again, despite his previous unsuccessful experiences with running independent record labels. He launched a new recording label called Mortal Records, which would serve as the vehicle for releasing his own music and potentially that of other artists.

This decision to return to label ownership, after the failures of both incarnations of Numa Records, might seem surprising, but it likely reflected both Gary's desire for creative control and independence, and perhaps also the changed landscape of the music industry in the digital age, where independent labels faced different challenges and opportunities than they had in the 1980s and early 1990s.

The establishment of Mortal Records demonstrated that he remained committed to maintaining as much control as possible over his creative output and business affairs, even if previous attempts at independence had not succeeded, suggesting either considerable optimism about his ability to make such an arrangement work or a lack of attractive alternatives in terms of major label interest that would have provided the financial and promotional support that comes with such deals.

Also in 2005, after several of his friends and colleagues were killed in unrelated flying accidents, he gave up flying. In an interview four years later Gary said, "I loved going to air shows, you'd bond really tightly with your team mates–it's an extreme thing to be doing, and you trust your life to them. And then it ended. I'd turn up and not know anyone. It got depressing. I'd sit down in the pilot's tent and there'd be all these people I'd not recognise. You'd look forward to someone turning up to have a chat with them, and they'd be dead."

His company Numanair had continued operating but after thirty-one years, with Numan and his family emigrating to America, it was dissolved on 18th June 2013.

On 13th March 2006, Numan released *Jagged*, which represented his fifteenth solo studio album and marked another chapter in his ongoing creative renaissance. The release was supported by an extensive promotional campaign and touring schedule that demonstrated Numan's continued commitment to connecting with audiences through live performance and his recognition of the importance of creating multiple touchpoints with fans around a new release.

An album launch gig was staged at The Forum, the well-known music venue located in Kentish Town, London (previously called the Town And Country Club), on 18th March 2006, just five days after the album's official release date. This launch event served to celebrate the album's appearance and to perform the new material for fans and media in a high-profile London setting that would generate coverage and excitement around the release.

Following the gig, Numan embarked upon an ambitious touring schedule that encompassed the UK, Europe, and the United States, all in support of *Jagged*. This extensive touring demonstrated both Gary's determination to promote the album properly and his confidence that there existed audiences across multiple territories who were interested in experiencing his new material in a live setting.

In keeping with contemporary promotional practices and the growing importance of online presence and digital marketing, Numan also launched a dedicated website specifically for *Jagged*. This website served to showcase the album, providing information about the release including track listings, background information about the album's creation, and other content designed to engage fans and generate interest in the new material. The creation of a specific album website, separate from any general Gary Numan online presence, underscored the importance being placed on this particular release and the desire to create a focused promotional platform.

Additionally, Numan made plans to capitalise on interest in his back catalogue and archive material by arranging to have his 1981 farewell concert issued on DVD by November

2006. This concert, which had taken place at Wembley Arena and marked what was supposed to be Numan's retirement from live performance, had previously been released on VHS under the title *Micromusic*, but this forthcoming DVD release would make it available in a modern format with improved picture and sound quality, allowing a new generation of fans to experience this historic performance whilst also providing longtime fans with an upgraded version of a concert they might already own in the outdated VHS format.

Furthermore, plans were made to release a DVD version of the *Jagged* album launch gig that had taken place at The Forum in Kentish Town. This would allow fans who had not been able to attend the launch event in person to experience the performance, whilst also providing those who had attended with a permanent document of the evening. The decision to film and release both historic archive material and contemporary performances demonstrated Gary's understanding of the multiple revenue streams available to artists and the appetite among his fanbase for both new material and documentation of his live performances across different eras of his career.

Please Push No More

In December 2006, Numan undertook yet another touring commitment, this time staging a brief "Classic Album" tour focused specifically on *Telekon*, his 1980 album which had been his final chart-topping album release and which represented the conclusion of what he retrospectively termed the "Machine" era of his career. This tour format, often pushed for by promoters, where artists perform a classic album in its entirety, had become increasingly popular as a way for established artists to celebrate significant releases from their back catalogue whilst providing fans with a unique concert experience focused on a specific body of work rather than the usual mixture of hits and new material. Not to say, increased ticket sales.

The *Telekon* "Classic Album" tour consisted of performances at several significant venues across the UK. These included Rock City, a well-known music venue located in Nottingham that had hosted countless significant performances by alternative and rock artists over the years; the Kentish Town Forum in London, the same venue where the *Jagged* launch gig had taken place earlier in the year, demonstrating the venue's importance as a regular performance space for Numan; and Club Academy, a venue associated with the Manchester Academy complex, bringing the tour to another major city in the UK music scene.

This brief tour saw Numan celebrate and revisit material from a creatively and commercially significant period of his career whilst also maintaining his visibility and connection with audiences during a year that had already seen substantial touring in support of *Jagged*.

In April 2007, twenty-one-year-old Birmingham born Ade Fenton released his debut solo studio album titled *Artificial Perfect*, described as a new industrial and electronic music label. Numan played a significant role in this release, contributing lead vocals to four separate tracks on the album, demonstrating his willingness to continue collaborative

125

work with other artists and producers working in electronic and industrial music territories that aligned with his own current musical direction.

The four tracks on which Numan performed lead vocals were "The Leather Sea," "Slide Away," "Recall" and "Healing." The latter track was selected as the first single to be extracted and released from the *Artificial Perfect* album, presumably because it was considered the most commercially viable or radio-friendly of the collaborations, or because it best represented the overall aesthetic and sound of the album. This choice to lead with a Numan-featuring track as the debut single from Fenton's album underscored Numan's value as a collaborator, with his distinctive voice and name recognition being considered assets that could help launch a new artist's career and generate interest in the album.

Following the release of "Healing," a second single, "The Leather Sea" was subsequently released in the UK on 30th July 2007. This was another of the tracks featuring Numan's lead vocals and also made the charts. Not only was this a great success for an emerging artist but for Numan, it demonstrated that his collaborations could still generate commercial interest.

It could be argued that the choice to release two Numan-featuring tracks as the first two singles from *Artificial Perfect* indicated the extent to which Numan's participation was considered central to the album's commercial prospects and the label's strategy for establishing Fenton as a solo artist in his own right.

In spring 2008, Numan undertook and successfully completed a fifteen-date tour spanning the UK and Ireland, with all performances selling out entirely, demonstrating the strength of audience interest in his work and his enduring appeal as a live performer.

This tour followed the same "Classic Album" format the Telekon tour had undertaken in December 2006, but this time the focus was on *Replicas*, his groundbreaking 1979 album that had reached number one on the UK charts and launched him to mainstream fame.

During each performance on this tour, Numan played the entire *Replicas* album in its proper sequence from beginning to end, allowing audiences to experience this seminal work as a complete artistic statement. The tour went beyond simply performing the album tracks, however, as Numan also included all the music from the *Replicas* era that had not appeared on the album itself, including B-sides and other material from that creative period, providing fans with a comprehensive experience of this pivotal moment in his career.

The successful tour, with its complete sell-out status across all fifteen dates, reflected and was part of a broader cultural phenomenon—the resurging popularity of electropop music in the UK during this period. Electronic pop music, which had dominated the early 1980s before giving way to other trends, was experiencing a significant revival, with new artists working in electronic pop styles achieving commercial success and older electronic acts finding renewed interest in their work. Numan's tour both benefited from and contributed to this resurgent interest in electronic music, positioning him not as a nostalgic heritage act trading purely on past glories but as an artist whose pioneering work was being recognised as foundational to contemporary electronic music trends.

The timing of the tour held particular significance beyond simply capitalising on the electropop revival, as it coincided with two important personal and professional anniversaries for Numan. 2008 marked his fiftieth birthday, a milestone that represented half a century of life and three decades as a professional musician. Additionally, 2008 marked the thirtieth anniversary of the original release of *Replicas*, making it an ideal moment to celebrate and revisit this album that had been so crucial to his breakthrough and to the broader development of electronic pop music. These dual anniversaries gave the tour additional resonance and provided a framework for reflecting on Numan's career trajectory and lasting influence.

In November 2007, some months before this successful tour would take place, Numan had confirmed through his official website that he was planning to work on a new studio album throughout 2008. At that stage, the album carried the working title of Splinter, though working titles are often changed before final release and represent provisional labels used during the creative process rather than definitive choices. However, Numan indicated that work on this new album would need to wait until after he had completed two other projects that were occupying his time and creative energies.

The first of these projects was a remixed version of *Jagged*, his 2006 album, released under the title *Jagged Edge*. The second project that needed completion before work could properly commence on the new album was a compilation CD of previously unreleased songs drawn from his previous three studio albums. This collection gathered together material that had been recorded during those album sessions but which had not made it onto the final released versions, whether because of running time constraints, aesthetic decisions, or other considerations. This compilation would eventually be released in 2011 under the title *Dead Son Rising*, though that release date was some years later than originally anticipated, with various factors delaying its completion and release.

Once these two projects were completed, Numan would be free to focus his full attention on creating new material for what would become his next proper studio album. However, the process of creating this album would prove considerably more protracted than the initial 2007 announcement might have suggested.

The album, which retained elements of its working title but emerged with the fuller title of *Splinter (Songs From A Broken Mind)*, was not released until 2013. This represented a gap of five years between the announcement that work would begin and the album's eventual release, and seven years since the release of *Jagged*.

This extended timeline likely reflected both the care and attention Numan wished to invest in the album and possibly various personal and professional challenges that may

have delayed its completion, though the lengthy gestation period would ultimately prove worthwhile when the album received widespread critical acclaim upon its eventual release.

Resurrection

Numan had scheduled and was prepared to perform a small number of live dates in America during April 2010, with appearances that included what would have been a high-profile performance at the Coachella Valley Music and Arts Festival, one of America's most prestigious and widely attended music festivals, which takes place annually in Indio, California.

However, these planned performances had to be cancelled due to circumstances entirely beyond Numan's or the promoters' control. Air travel throughout Europe was halted and grounded as a consequence of the volcanic ash cloud that resulted from the eruption of the Eyjafjallajökull volcano in Iceland. The massive ash cloud created hazardous conditions for aircraft and led to the largest disruption of air travel in Europe since the Second World War, affecting countless flights and stranding passengers across the continent.

Instead, as a result and the subsequent rescheduling process, the tour was not only postponed to later in the year but was actually expanded beyond its original scope, with additional dates added. What emerged was branded as the Pleasure Principle 30th Anniversary Tour, focusing on Gary's landmark 1979 album in similar fashion to the Replicas tour he had undertaken in 2008.

The American and Mexican dates for this expanded tour commenced on 17th October 2010, at a venue called Firestone Live located in Orlando, Florida. This October start date represented a delay of six months from the originally scheduled April performances, but the expansion of the tour and the "Classic Album" format focusing on *The Pleasure Principle* in its entirety more than compensated for the disappointment of the cancelled spring dates and offered American audiences a more comprehensive and musically focused concert experience than the original smaller run of dates might have provided.

The Pleasure Principle 30th Anniversary Tour concept was not limited to North America, and in May 2011, Numan took the tour to Australia. The Australian dates held particular significance as Numan was joined on the bill by Severed Heads, an Australian electronic band with a long and respected history in experimental and industrial electronic music.

The participation of Severed Heads as support act was especially notable and significant because the band had actually retired from performing and had not been active as a touring entity. However, they made the decision to come out of retirement especially for these shows with Numan, presumably because of their respect for his work and influence, the significance of the tour celebrating such a landmark album, or the opportunity to perform for audiences who would appreciate their own contributions to electronic music.

It testified to his stature within the electronic music community and the regard in which he was held by fellow artists, whilst also providing Australian audiences with the opportunity to see a reformed version of an important local electronic act they might have thought they would never have the chance to experience live again.

****

Numan contributed his distinctive vocals to the track "My Machines" on *Gloss Drop*, the second studio album by the American experimental rock band Battles, which was released in 2011. This collaboration represented an interesting

pairing, bringing together Numan's established electronic sensibilities with Battles' complex, rhythmically intricate approach to experimental rock, and it demonstrated the continued willingness of younger, critically acclaimed bands to seek out Numan as a collaborator, recognising both his iconic voice and his credibility within experimental and alternative music circles.

The relationship between Numan and Battles extended beyond simply this studio collaboration, as Numan was subsequently chosen by Battles to perform at the ATP (All Tomorrow's Parties) Nightmare Before Christmas festival, an event that the band co-curated in December 2011. The festival took place in Minehead, England, at the distinctive Butlin's holiday camp that had become the regular home for ATP festivals.

Being invited to perform at a festival curated by Battles represented a significant honour and mark of respect, as curator-selected line-ups typically reflect the curating artists' particular tastes and the acts they consider most significant or interesting. This invitation positioned Numan within a context of experimental and alternative music rather than as a purely nostalgic or heritage act, underlining his continuing relevance to contemporary musicians working in adventurous territory.

Numan's sixteenth solo studio album, *Dead Son Rising*, was released on 16th September 2011. This release, which collected previously unreleased material from earlier album sessions as had been announced years earlier, was supported by a full UK tour, though the touring schedule was structured in an unusual manner.

Rather than undertaking a single continuous tour, the dates were split into two separate halves or legs. The first leg ran from 15th to 21st September 2011, beginning just one day before the album's release and running for approximately one week. Following this initial run of concerts, there was a substantial gap of several months before the five-day run of dates of the second leg of the tour from 7th to 11th December 2011. Maybe this was due to venue availability, Numan's own schedule and commitments, or a strategic decision to maintain promotional visibility for the album across a longer period rather than concentrating all touring activity into a single intensive period.

Both legs of the Dead Son Rising tour featured the same support act, with Welsh solo artist Jayce Lewis opening the shows throughout. In an interview conducted during the course of the tour, Numan spoke highly of Lewis, describing him as "one of the most popular" support acts with whom he had toured. This was significant praise, given that Numan had toured with numerous support acts over his three-decade-plus career, and it suggested that Lewis had succeeded in connecting with Numan's audiences in ways that generated genuine enthusiasm rather than simply being tolerated as an obligatory warm-up act before the main attraction.

Numan also chose to share aspects of his touring experience directly with fans by publishing portions of his tour diary online following the conclusion of the Dead Son Rising tour. These diary entries offered insights into the day-to-day realities of touring, Numan's reflections on the performances and audiences, and personal observations about returning to various cities and venues.

This practice of sharing tour diaries represented a form of direct connection with fans that the internet had made possible, allowing artists to bypass traditional media gatekeepers and communicate their experiences and thoughts directly to interested audiences.

Beyond his musical activities, Numan also ventured into film work again during 2011, though in a rather different capacity than his earlier film scoring work. He provided narration for *Odokuro*, the fifth short film in the *ChimeraScope* series created by Aurelio Voltaire, a Cuban-American musician and filmmaker known for his work spanning music, animation, and various visual media. Numan's narration added an atmospheric, authoritative, or characterful vocal presence to the film, lending his distinctive voice to Voltaire's visual storytelling.

Odokuro proved to be a successful film by the standards of the short film and film festival circuit, winning twelve awards at various festivals and competitions. The film was selected for screening at numerous film festivals between 2011 and 2013, receiving substantial exposure on the festival circuit over a two-year period.

This represented a significant achievement for a short film, as selection at multiple festivals and the accumulation of twelve awards indicated that *Odokuro* had connected with festival programmers, judges, and audiences across many different contexts and had been recognised for its qualities across a sustained period.

Numan's participation in this successful project demonstrated his willingness to lend his talents to different artistic media beyond purely musical endeavours and his openness to collaborations with artists working in different creative fields.

Numan's seventeenth solo studio album, *Splinter (Songs From A Broken*

Mind), was released on 14th October 2013, and it represented a significant commercial and critical breakthrough after many years of operating outside the mainstream charts. The album achieved a position within the UK Top 20, marking the first time in thirty years that a new Numan studio album had reached this level of chart success.

This was particularly remarkable given the extended period Numan had spent in the commercial wilderness during the late 1980s and much of the 1990s, and it demonstrated that his critical and commercial rehabilitation, which had been building gradually since *Sacrifice* in 1994, had now translated into genuine mainstream chart success rather than merely cult appreciation or critical respect.

The release of *Splinter (Songs From A Broken Mind)* was supported by an exceptionally extensive and geographically diverse touring schedule that demonstrated both Numan's commitment to promoting the album properly and the existence of substantial audiences for his work across multiple territories worldwide.

The initial touring schedule encompassed the United States, Canada, the United Kingdom, and Ireland, representing a comprehensive coverage of English-speaking markets where Numan had historically maintained fanbases.

Rather than concluding after this initial run of territories, however, the touring schedule continued throughout 2014, expanding to include Israel, New Zealand, Australia, and various European countries as Gary spent much of both 2013 and 2014 on the road, travelling between continents and performing in front of audiences across the globe.

A further leg focusing specifically on the United States took place in late 2014, indicating that American audiences' response to the album and the earlier US shows had been sufficiently positive to justify returning to that market for additional performances within the same album cycle.

In June 2014, during the extended touring period supporting Splinter, Numan found time to collaborate once again with Jayce Lewis. This collaboration resulted in the track "Redesign," which originally featured on *Protafield*, a studio album credited to Lewis's band Nemesis. The track showcased the creative rapport that had developed between the two artists. The album on which "Redesign" appeared would later be re-released in 2018 as a special edition, though this time it was issued under Jayce Lewis's solo name rather than the Nemesis band credit, suggesting a shift in how Lewis was positioning himself professionally or perhaps indicating that Nemesis had been essentially a solo project operating under a band name.

Also in 2014, Numan ventured into the world of video game music, an increasingly significant sector of the entertainment industry and one where electronic music and atmospheric composition played crucial roles. He provided lead vocals for the song "Long Way Down," which had been composed by Masafumi Takada, a respected Japanese video game composer, with lyrics written by Rich Dickerson.

The track was created specifically for *The Evil Within*, a survival horror video game that sought to create an atmosphere of dread and tension, making Numan's distinctive, slightly detached vocal style and his associations with dystopian themes entirely appropriate for the project. *The Evil Within* was released on 14th October 2014, coincidentally exactly one year to the day after *Splinter (Songs From A Broken Mind)* had been released, creating an odd symmetry in Numan's release schedule.

In November 2014, during a brief break in his extensive international touring commitments, Numan performed a special one-off live show in London at the Hammersmith Apollo, a prestigious and historically significant venue that had hosted countless important performances over its long history.

The show was structured as a sold-out, standalone performance rather than part of a regular tour, giving it a special event quality that distinguished it from typical tour dates. The fact that the show sold out entirely demonstrated the strength of demand for Numan's live performances in his home city, even after the extensive touring he had been undertaking throughout 2013 and 2014.

The choice of support act for this special London performance was particularly significant and somewhat surprising. Gang of Four, the influential English post-punk band who had emerged from the same late-1970s milieu as Numan, but who had taken a radically different musical direction—combining angular, politically charged lyrics with stripped-down, funk-influenced guitar work rather than embracing synthesisers—were selected to open the show.

Gang of Four represented a different strand of post-punk innovation than Numan did, and their presence on the bill created an interesting contrast and dialogue between two different approaches to moving beyond punk's initial assault. The pairing suggested mutual respect between artists who had emerged from the same historical moment but had pursued very different artistic paths, and it positioned Numan firmly within the post-punk tradition rather than as simply an electronic pop artist, underlining his credibility within the broader alternative music community.

That Gang of Four, themselves a respected and influential band with their own substantial legacy, were willing to serve as support act for Numan testified to his restored stature within British music and the recognition that his innovations and influence were deserving of respect from his peers and contemporaries.

Numan collaborated with VOWWS, a Los Angeles-based Australian duo, contributing to the track "Losing Myself in You" which appeared on their debut studio album titled *The Great Sun*. This collaboration represented another instance of Numan working with younger artists operating in industrial and electronic territories, lending his distinctive vocal presence and name recognition to an emerging act's first full-length release and helping to introduce them to his own fanbase whilst also demonstrating his continued engagement with contemporary developments in electronic and industrial music.

On 6th May 2016, Numan participated in what was undoubtedly one of the most prestigious collaborations of his career when he appeared as one of several collaborators on *Electronica 2: The Heart of Noise*, the eighteenth studio album by Jean-Michel Jarre, the legendary French electronic music pioneer whose work had been hugely influential in establishing electronic music as a serious artistic form and who had achieved enormous commercial success across multiple decades.

The track on which Numan appeared was titled "Here For You" and significantly, it was co-written by both Jarre and Numan rather than Gary simply providing vocals to a Jarre composition. This co-writing credit indicated a genuine creative collaboration between two major figures in electronic music from different generations and national traditions, representing a meeting of minds between one of electronic music's founding fathers and one of its most important second-generation innovators.

Just four days later, on 10th May 2016, Numan received official recognition of his innovations and contributions to electronic music when he was named as the recipient of the 2016 Moog Innovation Award by Moog Music, the company founded by synthesiser pioneer Robert Moog and responsible for creating some of the most important and influential synthesisers in the history of electronic music.

The Moog Innovation Award represented recognition from the very heart of synthesiser culture and technology, acknowledging Numan's role in demonstrating the artistic and commercial possibilities of synthesiser-based music and his innovative approaches to using electronic instruments.

Coming from Moog Music specifically, this award carried particular weight and significance, as it represented acknowledgment from the manufacturers of the very instruments that had made Numan's music possible, recognition that he had used their technology in genuinely innovative and influential ways.

On 18th May 2017, Numan received another significant honour when he was presented with an Ivor Novello Inspiration Award by the British Academy of Songwriters, Composers, and Authors, one of the most respected institutions in British music.

The Ivor Novello Awards, named after the Welsh composer and entertainer, are among the most prestigious honours in British music, focusing specifically on songwriting and composition rather than commercial success or performance.

They are awarded by the professional songwriting community to recognise excellence in musical creation.

The Inspiration Award specifically recognises artists whose work has inspired and influenced other songwriters and composers, making it a particularly appropriate honour for Numan given the countless artists across multiple genres who have cited his influence.

This award represented recognition from his peers and fellow professionals in the British music industry, for his contributions to British songwriting and his influence on subsequent generations of composers.

In 2017, Numan released the single "My Name Is Ruin," which served as the lead single from his forthcoming album and helped to generate anticipation and interest in the new material. The single's release was followed by a European tour that took place in September 2017, allowing audiences across Europe to experience Numan's live performance and hear new material from the forthcoming album alongside established favourites from his extensive catalogue.

The End Of Things

Numan's eighteenth solo studio album, *Savage (Songs From A Broken World)*, was released on 15th September 2017, during the European tour. The album represented another major commercial and critical success, charting at number two in the UK album charts.

It was Gary's highest chart position for a studio album since *Telekon* had reached number one in 1980, an astonishing gap of thirty-seven years between top-three chart positions. The fact that *Savage (Songs From A Broken World)* reached number two demonstrated his commercial and critical renaissance, which had been building since the mid-1990s and had accelerated with Splinter's top twenty position in 2013. It had now reached a point where he was once again competing at the very highest levels of the UK album charts, achieving positions that would have seemed impossible during the difficult decades of the 1980s and 1990s.

Later in 2017, Numan received yet another award recognising his contributions and legacy, when he was named as the winner of the 2017 T3

Tech Legends Award. *T3* is a technology and lifestyle magazine, and their Tech Legends Award recognised figures who had made significant contributions at the intersection of technology and popular culture.

For Numan, whose entire career had been built around exploring the artistic possibilities of electronic music technology and whose work had always engaged with questions about technology's role in contemporary life, this award from a technology-focused publication represented particularly appropriate recognition.

It acknowledged that his significance extended beyond purely musical contributions to encompass his role in demonstrating how technology could be used creatively and his prescient explorations of themes relating to technology, identity, and contemporary life that had only become more relevant as digital technology increasingly shaped every aspect of modern existence.

Numan's nineteenth solo studio album, titled *Intruder*, was released on 21st May 2021, representing his continued creative productivity and relevance well into the fifth decade of his professional career.

Prior to the full album's release, the title track "Intruder" was released as a single on 11th January 2021, some four months before the album appeared, serving to generate anticipation and interest in the forthcoming full-length release and giving audiences an early taste of the album's sonic direction and thematic concerns.

Numan engaged in substantive discussion about the album's creation and the ideas behind it with writer Guy Mankowski, a cultural commentator who had written extensively about British popular music and alternative culture.

Mankowski had included a chapter focusing specifically on Numan's legacy and influence in his book titled Albion's Secret History: Snapshots of England's Pop Rebels and Outsiders, a work that examined various figures in English popular music who had operated outside the mainstream or challenged conventional approaches.

The discussion between Numan and Mankowski about *Intruder's* genesis took place as part of an interview series on influential English artists that was produced for Zer0 Books, a publisher known for their politically engaged and culturally analytical publications.

This context—being discussed as part of a series on influential English artists and having a chapter devoted to his legacy in a book about English pop rebels and outsiders—positioned Numan firmly within a tradition of British artists who had challenged conventions and operated according to their own vision rather than following established commercial formulas.

Following the release of *Intruder*, Numan undertook an extensive touring schedule to promote the album and perform the new material for audiences. His US Intruder tour took place in late 2021 and continued into early 2022, representing a substantial commitment to the American market and recognition of the significant fanbase he had built there over the decades. Following the conclusion of the American dates, Numan returned to the United Kingdom to undertake a seventeen-venue UK tour that ran between late April and late May 2022. This touring schedule, spanning multiple months and two continents with dozens of performances, demonstrated Numan's continued stamina and commitment to live performance at an age when many of his contemporaries had either retired entirely or limited themselves to occasional, carefully selected appearances.

In October 2023, Numan undertook a distinctive and unusual concert series that represented a significant departure from his typical large-venue performances and electronic sound. He performed a series of eight acoustic gigs, reimagining and reinterpreting songs from across his extensive repertoire in a new way, stripping them of their characteristic electronic arrangements and presenting them in acoustic form. These performances took place in smaller, more intimate settings than the arenas and large concert halls he typically played, creating opportunities for closer, more direct connection with audiences and allowing the songs to be heard in radically different contexts than those in which they were originally conceived and recorded.

The locations chosen for these acoustic performances were notably diverse and often architecturally or historically significant spaces rather than conventional music venues. Among the venues were Wylam Brewery in Newcastle upon Tyne, an industrial brewery space that provided an atmospheric setting; Manchester Cathedral, a magnificent Gothic cathedral dating back to the medieval period, whose sacred architecture and exceptional acoustics created a particularly unusual and striking context for Numan's typically dystopian and secular material; and the Church of St John-at-Hackney in London, another historic church building whose ecclesiastical setting provided fascinating counterpoint to the technological and science-fictional themes that characterise much of Numan's work.

The choice to perform in breweries and churches rather than traditional music venues suggested a desire to create unique experiences and to explore how his material might function in spaces with very different acoustic properties and cultural associations than those in which it was typically heard.

In February 2024, Numan announced plans for a major UK tour that would celebrate a significant milestone in his career—the forty-fifth anniversary of the 1979 studio albums *Replicas* and *The Pleasure Principle*, the two releases that had established him as a major force in British popular music and which remained his most influential and celebrated works.

The tour was scheduled to take place between 19th May and 1st June 2024, representing a concentrated two-week period of intensive touring. The itinerary included performances in eleven different cities across England, Scotland, and Wales, ensuring comprehensive coverage of the United Kingdom. The cities included on the tour routing were Norwich, Sheffield, Glasgow, Newcastle upon Tyne, Manchester, London, Bristol, Cardiff, Bournemouth, Birmingham, and Nottingham.

In March 2025, Numan appeared as a featured vocalist on new material by another artist, demonstrating his continued willingness to collaborate with musicians working in electronic music territories. He contributed lead vocals to a track titled "Polished Chrome (The Friend Pt. 1)" which appeared on a new studio album released by Chris Liebing, a highly respected German techno DJ and producer who had been a significant figure in the techno scene for decades.

The collaboration brought together Numan's distinctive vocal style and his long history in electronic music with Liebing's more dancefloor-oriented techno production, creating an interesting fusion of different strands within electronic music culture. The track's title, with its reference to "polished chrome" and its designation as "The Friend Pt. 1," seemed to echo some of Numan's own recurring themes and imagery, suggesting a collaboration that was conceptually as well as sonically considered.

On 28th June 2025, Numan achieved what represented a notable milestone in his long career when he made his debut performance at the Glastonbury Festival, widely considered the most prestigious and culturally significant music festival in the United Kingdom. He performed on the Park Stage, one of the festival's several major stages and a venue that typically hosts established acts with significant cult followings and critical respect.

The fact that Numan had reached the age of sixty-seven and enjoyed a career spanning more than forty-five years before making his Glastonbury debut was itself remarkable, representing an unusually late first appearance at a festival that many major British artists play multiple times throughout their careers.

His debut performance at Glastonbury in 2025, coming after decades of critical and commercial ups and downs, after years of being dismissed by the music press, after a remarkable late-career renaissance that had seen him achieve his highest chart positions in decades, represented a form of validation and acceptance by the British music establishment.

Glastonbury, known for championing both emerging artists and established legends, had finally extended an invitation to an artist whose influence on British electronic music was undeniable but who had long operated somewhat outside the festival's traditional booking patterns. The performance allowed Numan to bring his music to the Glastonbury audience, many of whom might be experiencing his work live for the first time, and it positioned him firmly within the canon of significant British artists whose presence at Glastonbury represents acknowledgment of their lasting importance to British popular music culture.

Gary's appearance represented far more than simply another festival booking or another item to add to an already extensive touring curriculum vitae. It stood as a profound symbol of vindication, of artistic perseverance rewarded, of a career that had travelled the full distance from the extraordinary heights of late-1970s chart dominance, through the deep valleys of critical dismissal and commercial failure, and back again to a position of respect, influence, and renewed success that few artists who experience such dramatic declines ever manage to achieve.

That a man of sixty-seven, who had first topped the charts when Margaret Thatcher had only just entered Downing Street, should be standing on one of British music's most prestigious stages nearly half a century later, his artistic reputation not merely intact but arguably enhanced, his influence on contemporary music widely acknowledged and celebrated, speaks to something rare and valuable in popular music: the triumph of integrity over expediency, of artistic vision over commercial calculation, of stubborn persistence over the easier option of graceful retirement. Furthermore his performance was considered one of the standout acts of the entire weekend.

****

The arc of Numan's career contains lessons that extend well beyond the specifics of his individual journey. His story demonstrates that critical opinion, however confidently expressed and however dismissive, is not the final arbiter of artistic value or cultural significance.

The British music press that savaged his work throughout the 1980s has been proven comprehensively wrong by history; the innovations they dismissed as cold, mechanical, and emotionally sterile are now recognised as pioneering contributions that opened pathways countless subsequent artists have explored. His experience shows that commercial decline, however precipitous and however demoralising, need not represent the end of a meaningful artistic career.

The years Numan spent in the wilderness, releasing albums that barely troubled the charts, playing to diminishing audiences, accumulating debt whilst watching artists he had influenced surpass him commercially—these difficult years did not break him or force him to abandon his vision, and they ultimately gave way to a renaissance that has brought him greater critical respect and arguably deeper artistic satisfaction than his initial burst of fame ever provided.

Numan's refusal to compromise, his determination to follow his artistic instincts regardless of whether they aligned with prevailing fashions or commercial wisdom, has been vindicated in the most satisfying way possible. The darker, more industrial direction he pursued from *Sacrifice* onwards, the exploration of more personal themes including his atheism and his psychological struggles, the commitment to making music that expressed his genuine preoccupations rather than calculating what might achieve radio play—all of these choices, which seemed commercially suicidal at the time, have proven to be precisely what allowed him to connect with new generations of listeners and to create work of lasting value.

The remarkable chart performances of *Splinter*, *Savage*, and *Intruder*, achieving positions that would have seemed impossible during his difficult decades, demonstrate that audiences ultimately respond to authenticity and conviction, even if that response sometimes takes years or decades to manifest.

Perhaps most importantly, Numan's career stands as testament to the value of artistic courage and the rewards of persistence in the face of adversity. He could have given up during the difficult years of the late 1980s and 1990s when nothing seemed to work, when each new release brought fresh disappointments, when the money ran out and the critics remained hostile.

He could have compromised his vision, attempted to recreate the formula that had brought him success in 1979, or chased whatever trends seemed commercially viable at any given moment. That he did neither, that he continued making music according to his own lights whilst absorbing influences that genuinely interested him rather than cynically adopting fashionable sounds, allowed him to maintain artistic integrity whilst ultimately finding his way back to commercial success and critical respect.

As Gary Numan approaches his seventieth year, still touring, still recording, still exploring new creative territories and collaborating with younger artists, his career stands as one of the most remarkable in British popular music.

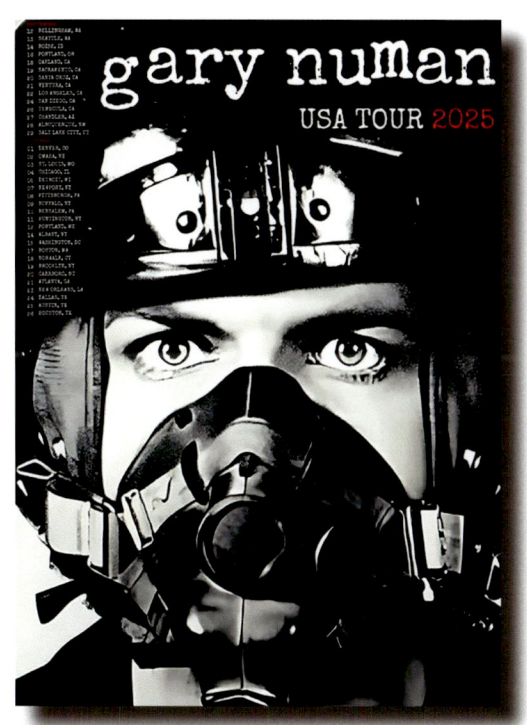

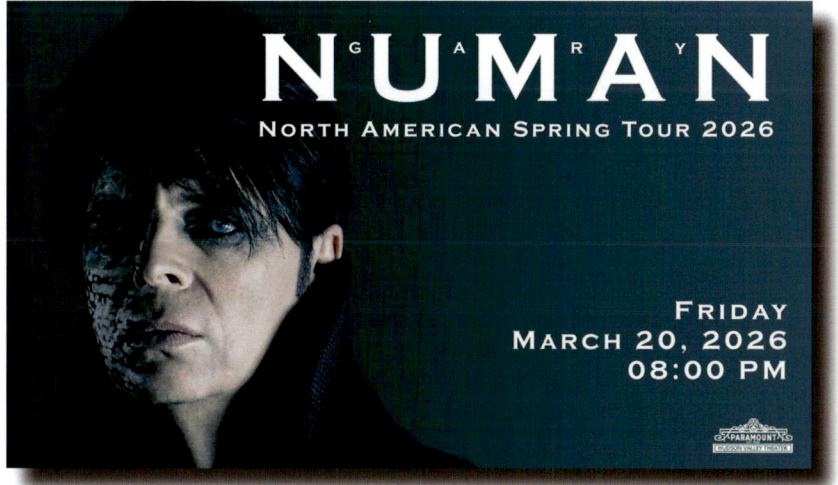

143